Good News!

Sermons of Hope for Today's Families

GOOD NEWS!

Sermons of Hope for Today's Families

JEREMIAH A. WRIGHT, JR.

Edited by Jini M. Kilgore

JUDSON PRESS
PUBLISHERS SINCE 1824
VALLEY FORGE, PA

Good News! Sermons of Hope for Today's Families

Library of Congress Cataloging-in-Publication Data
Wright, Jeremiah A., Jr.
Good News! : sermons of hope for today's families / Jeremiah A. Wright, Jr. ; edited by Jini Kilgore Ross.
p. cm.
Includes bibliographical references.
ISBN 0-8170-1236-2 (pbk. : alk. paper)
1. Afro-Americans—Religion—Sermons. 2. Afro-American families—Sermons. 3. Sermons, American—Afro-Americans authors. I. Ross, Jini Kilgore, 1948- . II. Title.
BR563.N4W66 1995
248.4—dc20 95-9572

Printed in the U.S.A.

Fifth printing, 2007.

Dedication

This work is prayerfully and gratefully dedicated to my wife, Ramah. God has given me more than a companion in allowing me to share life with her. God has given me insight into the deepest meanings of being a family by blessing me with such a powerful soul mate.

Ramah has been both a wife and a mother. Ramah has been the embodiment of God's "Good News" in my life. Ramah has taught me the humility one feels when touched by the awesomeness of God's grace, and Ramah has shown me what Peter felt when the risen Lord bathed his former behavior with forgiveness!

I thank God for my wife who has shared with me and shown me what God had on God's mind when granting humankind the covenant of marriage; and to you, Ramah, I say from the bottom of my heart...

Thank you!
Rev. Jeremiah A. Wright, Jr.

Contents

Foreword

The African American Family: In the Beginning

The African American family continues to be the subject of extensive investigation and analysis. The conclusions drawn from many of these sociological, economical, and psychological examinations emerge as a litany of pathologies and negative assessments. The critical issues and concerns facing the black family cannot be trivialized or addressed through simplistic and reductionistic formulas and programs. Nevertheless, any engagement of the issues confronting African American families must begin with an affirmation and celebration of the strengths and accomplishments of our families.

In spite of numerous inhospitable circumstances and societal obstacles, the black family has been the nurturing womb and development nexus that has led to the formation of sane, courageous, centered, and competent persons. The African American family has not only cared for her own, but all others within her arms' reach. Reflecting on the greatness of our households establishes the standards for discerning devastations and compels us to recognize where and when we have meandered in missed majesty.

Jeremiah A. Wright, Jr., is a pastor/scholar who with passion and perceptive insights speaks healing and hope to relationships and families. Our discussion of the family and the nature of persons has always commenced with reflection on God's original intent, desire, decree, and design.

The combined testimonies of the creative event recorded in Genesis provide a core principle related to God's intent and desire for human relationships, the developing family, and the human community. Men and women are called into a relationship characterized by mutuality, reciprocity, and shared responsibility. As co-regents they are called to be "one." The original command given to humans is to be fruitful and to cultivate the earth. Fruitfulness and cultivation are charges to be life creating, life affirming, life encouraging, and life fostering. The call to be fruitful is expanded through a call to stewardship and faithful care of each other and the earth.

The call to faithfulness and fruitful stewardship is violated when we abdicate responsibility and surrender our minds, ways, and selves to the dictates of the snake. The snake represents the demonic forces in a free moral universe that invite our participation in that which is alien to the intent and desire of God. When we succumb to the snake, we depart from fruitfulness and enter the state of death. Death is a state of fragmentation and separation. It is fruitless existence that neither celebrates life nor births new life. Eating the fruit of the tree of knowledge is a fruitless act of the estranged who have embraced the fragmenting invitation of the demonic.

The Genesis creation narrative offers collected reflections about a self-giving God who ordains harmony, relatedness, and communion. In the beginning, we are one with God, one with ourselves, one with each other, and one with nature. When we surrender our majesty and are other-directed by the snake, brokenness invades the God-intended integration and harmonious relationships. Hiding in fear, we are separated from God. Ashamed of our bodies, we are separated from our true selves. Blaming and in conflict with our partners, we are separated from each other. Distanced from the garden, we are separated from nature.

As suggested in the third chapter of Genesis, this fragmentation has dire consequences for the family. Children become a pain, male-female relationships become hierarchical, care becomes irresponsible, and survival becomes a struggle.

I would note that the introduction of hierarchy (over-under, domination-subjugation) in relationships was a consequence of sin. Relationships modeled after hierarchical principles neither reflect God's intent nor the vision of the family restored in Jesus Christ. In the beginning, and in the Christ re-creation, children are not "pains" to be abused, neglected, and objectified, but rather gifts of God to be loved, nurtured, and equipped. Women are not weak bodies to be possessed, pitied, and put on a pedestal, but rather creative, fruitful partners; men are not controlling tyrants, but rather power-filled, caring lovers.

Too often the church glorifies the consequences of sin with a message that suggests the inferiority of women and the objectification of children. This is the message of the snake, not God. This shift from theology to "snakeology" contributes to the tragic and expanding abuse of women and children and the self-destruction of men. The sacralization of superiority and the divinization of dominance is a demonic approach to discipling the black male. Such an approach perpetuates male infancy and insults the strength of African American manhood. Black men are too strong and too wise to be seduced into being forever boys.

If we are to minister to the African American family, we must revisit the beginning and recognize the truth of God and the lie of the snake. We preach not what sin caused, but rather what God desired. Our witness is rooted in the liberating truth of Jesus Christ and not the oppressive falsehoods of the snake. We are empowered to tread upon the snake, to take up the snake, and to bear much fruit. In fact, you shall know them by their fruit.

Revisiting the beginning compels us to engage seriously our African heritage as a critical resource for ministering to the African American family. We should not expect persons from other cultures to provide the creative energy and substance for a liberating ministry to our families. A startling number of marriages in this nation end in divorce, and many of the remaining relationships are dysfunctional. Some are suggesting that the children of the African diaspora should stop divorcing each other and divorce those elements in our culture that breed so many broken and dysfunctional relationships.

When we revisit the beginning, we discover that fruitful existence began in Africa. Genesis reveals to us that the rivers of the garden flowed into the lands of Cush and his children. Current anthropology, archaeology, and genetics suggest that all humans living today descended from the same woman. This woman, mitochondrial "Eve," is described as a black-skinned, fruitful woman in sub-Saharan East Africa. All living persons today have the same ten thousandth great-grandmother, and she is African. One should not oversimplify the content of Scripture or genetic studies, and one should not make a simplistic connection between mitochondrial "Eve" and the "Eve" of Genesis. One can, however, establish both a theological and scientific basis for revisiting Africa as one develops resources for the African American family. This is not to romanticize the African family on either side of the Atlantic, but it is to suggest that there is great truth within. We could be well served by revisiting communal responsibility for children, the security and care provided by an extended family, respect for the elders, the co-regency of queen mothers and king fathers, the duty of fruitfulness for the well-being of community, and the transition and instruction provided by rites of passage.

The snake still entices us to embrace the lie, and some speak lies because they are cruelly deceived. Others speak lies because they have a vested interest in the maintenance of the lie. Still others are overcoming the serpent and being fruitful. These persons are healing brokenness and bringing forth life even in the midst of death.

I thank God for the many courageous men and women who are ministering to the African American family with truth.

I thank God for Jeremiah A. Wright, Jr. In this collection of sermons he speaks to the pain and promise in our relationships and families. With street savvy, revolutionary wisdom, liberating exegesis, and divine anointing, he ministers to all of us. The shared gifts of his mind, person, and spirit will challenge you, inspire you, teach you, convict you, and empower you. He speaks truth, and the truth will set you free.

JOHN W. KINNEY
Dean and Professor of Theology
The School of Theology of Virginia Union University

Acknowledgments

There are too many people to thank for making this volume possible. There are the obvious persons such as Rev. Jini Ross whose patience, persistence, and prodding brought this book into being; Ms. Janet Wright-Hall, my administrative assistant whose efficiency and attention to detail have kept me with some sense of order in my life; and Ms. Jeri Wright whose media ministry at Trinity UCC Chicago has provided the "rough drafts" from which these sermons were crafted.

In addition to the obvious persons, however, there are far too many others whose names I do not have space to mention! There are the families to whom I minister whose lives and whose "stories" make these messages come alive. There are the individuals who have let me into the private places of their lives as their pastor, and who have blessed me far more than I have helped them. They have shared both their pain and the power that God has given them in spite of their experiences.

I thank each person, each family, and each ministry that has shaped my angle of vision and given me the perspective that eventuated into the messages you now hold in your hand. My prayer is that as these servants of God have blessed my life, so may these sermons bless your life!

Jeremiah A. Wright, Jr.

I am indebted to a number of people who helped in the making of this book. I wish to thank my husband, Earl Ross, for his constant encouragement and patience. I also extend my thanks to the following persons and institutions in Houston, Texas, for their help in providing information for the footnotes contained in the book: Mrs. Juanita Nash, minister of music at Wheeler Avenue Baptist Church; the personnel in the Information and Research Department of the Houston Public Library; the librarians at the Smith Branch, Houston Public Library; and the personnel at the Shrine of the Black Madonna Cultural Center. I am grateful to Carolyn Neal for transcribing Dr. Wright's sermon tapes from which the book is composed. I extend hearty thanks to Mary M. Nicol, editorial manager and Victoria W. McGoey, editorial assistant at Judson Press for their careful attention to detail and quality. Most especially, I am grateful to God for the keen intellect, the anointed spirit, and the precious and powerful gift of preaching with which he has endowed Dr. Jeremiah A. Wright, Jr., and I thank Dr. Wright for allowing me to edit both this book and *What Makes You So Strong?* (Valley Forge, PA: Judson Press, 1993). My prayer is that you, the reader, will be blessed in your reading and discussions, and that the great cause of Jesus Christ will be furthered.

Jini Kilgore Ross

Introduction

by James A. Forbes, Jr.

The Sunday following Chicago's worst heat wave in recorded history, I was privileged to worship at Trinity United Church of Christ. Nearly five hundred people had perished in the wake of the intense heat, and the forecast was for more of the same. Yet the members of Trinity flocked to their newly dedicated edifice because family is supposed to gather for comfort and encouragement when disaster strikes. Over eight thousand parishioners and their friends made up the capacity crowds for the three services held that day. Some walked to church, others came by public transportation, many came by car, and a few were assisted from stretch limousines by their drivers. One thing they had in common was an eagerness to find a good seat in time to share the spirit of praise, healing, and renewal of hope. Every Sunday at Trinity is a family reunion, and the brothers and sisters expect to hear the good news that God's providential care will sustain them through whatever crisis another week might bring.

During the service, funeral plans were announced for one of the little boys who had died after being left in the sweltering heat of a day-care van. Two sisters, one of whom had donated a kidney to the other, were asked to stand so the congregation could see them. Infants were lifted into the air in ritual pride as an African element of Christian dedication. Members were encouraged to join hands as they were led into intercessory prayer. During the children's sermon, all the little ones gathered around the pastor were given opportunities to recite the memory verse of the month or to recall a favorite story out of African folklore. Throughout the worship, vibrant music seemed to transform the whole congregation into a spirit-filled mass gospel choir. By the end of the six o'clock service it was clear that the trend of recent months was continuing: nearly fifty new members had joined the church.

Why the phenomenal growth of this congregation? There may be many reasons, but one of them is that worshipers experience being part of an extended family of faith. The program activities, the preaching and teaching, the social services, and the witness for justice give evidence of serious substantive commitment to strengthening and supporting the family spirit.

A central feature in building the family spirit at Trinity is the preaching of Dr. Jeremiah Wright—one of the most creative, dynamic, and richly resourceful pulpiteers of our time. The collection of sermons included in this volume reveals the kind of preaching that enables a congregation to be a loving family of faith.

Readers of these sermons will see that there are no issues that are so hot or so controversial that they may not be addressed from the pulpit. Where there are conflicting theologies or sensitive moral and ethical dilemmas affecting the lives of the people, something ought to be said by the pastor of the people who struggle to live by the liberty and discipline of the gospel of Jesus Christ. In these sermons Dr. Wright seeks to model faithful wrestling with contemporary issues in light of the biblical heritage which is ours as the body of Christ.

Of equal significance is the inclusion of all sorts and conditions of family configurations. Dr. Wright does not approach his congregation as if only the traditional family has gained admission into the beloved community. There are no second-class citizens in this commonwealth of faith. His understanding of Christianity would question a ministry that is always tailor-made for so-called ideal circumstances. He does not assume that the form of a relationship always guarantees integrity or love. He holds out the prospect that grace will often show up in places and with people who have known disgrace. These sermons proclaim that it is precisely for this reason that the gospel is Good News for all of us.

In these sermons one will be struck by the language, images, illustrations, and style. Formality and careful attention to propriety are replaced by the way people talk when they are with the family. In this sense the colloquial style becomes the medium that embodies the message. Call it what it is, tell it like it is, because reality isn't always dressed up in "Sunday-go-to-meeting" attire. This is what I hear the pastor saying to his congregation as he comes before them wearing casual street clothes or assorted African robes.

Not every pastor will be able to wear this preacher's "armor" when bringing the message of the day. But no responsible Christian minister can ignore these issues or overlook the members who wrestle with them day by day. Each of us must find our own way to preach the gospel so that it will bring hope to all the brothers and sisters, mothers and fathers, singles and married, relatives and guardians, gays and straights, good and bad, blended and extended families.

If we bring to our preaching task the diligence, dedication, love, and courage reflected in these sermons, perhaps families will rush to get a good seat when the doors open.

JAMES A. FORBES, JR.
Senior Minister
The Riverside Church

How to Use the Devotional and Study Questions

For groups who want to discuss in depth the sermon topics in this book, a fifteen-minute devotional format accompanies each chapter, as well as ten study questions. The suggested format for the devotional and the study group sessions is included at the end of each chapter.

The devotional time can be lengthened to include a verbal summary of the sermon or the reading of selected passages from the sermon or the entire sermon. This can serve as a review before the study session begins. However, whether you have a summary review or not, encourage the participants to read the sermon before coming to class so the material will be familiar to everyone.

If the group is small, ask as many questions as will fit within your time frame. Larger groups can be divided into subgroups, with each one being assigned some of the questions. With several subgroups, the study time can be shortened so that twenty to thirty minutes are left at the end of the session to hear the answers from designated representatives from each of the groups. Some questions involve preparation and forethought prior to the class, and the leader might want to select discussion leaders ahead of time.

Good News for Married Folks

Genesis 41:45-52

Introduction

Joseph is one biblical model for manhood who needs to be lifted up over and over again for all our young African American males to see. He came from some adverse circumstances, but he did not let his circumstances circumscribe his possibilities. He overcame adversity and worked hard at becoming the best man he could possibly be.

When he was scarcely a teenager, he lost his mother, Rachel, when she died in childbirth. His papa, Jacob, was a rolling stone; he had children by four different women. It's in the Book (Genesis 35). Jacob had six boys and one girl by Leah; two boys by Rachel; two boys by Bilhah, Rachel's maid; and two other boys by Zilpah, Leah's maid. Papa was a rolling stone.

We're talking about a messed-up family! One of his half-brothers slept with one of his father's women.[1] And his old man had two problems. First, he had four women—one love ahead, one love behind, one in his arms, and one on his mind. Joseph's papa was a pistol. His second and main problem was that he was married to one woman and in love with another woman. It's in the Book (Genesis 29).

One strike Joseph had going against him was the home he came out of, the circumstances surrounding his upbringing, and the role models of manhood that he saw while he was a little boy. By the time he was seventeen, he had seen it all. Hated by his half-brothers, he was launched into the world from a dysfunctional family. He was cut off from all the support systems he had known as a child, even though those support systems were flawed and flaky.

In addition to his genealogical strike, he had a physiological as well as a sociological strike against him. Physiologically, Joseph was well built and good-looking.[2] Now, remember what a rolling stone his daddy had been. Remember the example his papa had set.

Add to his looks this sociological strike against him: his master's wife began to desire Joseph and asked him to go to bed with her. Look at Genesis 39:10. She asked Joseph day after day—and when he kept saying no, she framed him and had him incarcerated.

So Joseph had three strikes against him. He was from a dysfunctional family; he was handsome; and despite his efforts, his circumstances led to his being wrongly imprisoned. He became a victim of an unjust criminal system—falsely accused, like a lot of black men, lied on with the cards stacked against him and witnesses telling stories on him, thrown in jail and forgotten. Yet, Joseph did not let his circumstances circumscribe his possibilities.

Look at Joseph's Theology

Joseph was nothing like his daddy. Young brothers, don't you let anybody tell you that "'cause your daddy wasn't nothin' before you, you ain't gonna amount to nothin'." Look at Joseph. Don't let anybody tell you that because you come from a messed-up family, you're going be messed up. Look at Joseph. Don't let anybody tempt you with the lie that everything good *to* you is automatically good *for* you. Look at Joseph. Joseph did not let his genealogical, his physiological, or his sociological circumstances circumscribe his possibilities. His theology outweighed his genealogy, physiology, and sociology.

If somebody tells you that you can't make it because you come from a single-parent family, you tell that person, "So did Joseph. So did Jesse Jackson. So did Val Jordan."[3] God is a mother for the motherless and a father for the fatherless. If somebody tells you that you can't make it because you're black, you're too short, you're too tall, you're too nondescript, you're too light, you're too dark, you're too cute, you're too ugly, you tell that person that God can take you just as you are and get the glory out of your life. You say, "You're looking at the outside, but my God looks at the heart. He can take me and do just what he wants to with me, and there ain't nothin' you can do about it because he's got all power in his hands."

If somebody tells you that you can't make it because you're from the ghetto or you're from the country, you smile. Throw your head back, throw your chest out, and walk on by faith, knowing that you can do all things through Christ who strengthens you. If your theology is straight, God can get the glory out of your life. Joseph did not let his circumstances circumscribe his possibilities. He took what God gave him and used it to the best of his ability, and the Lord blessed his life. Joseph is one biblical model for manhood that needs to be lifted up over and over again for all our young African American brothers to see.

Joseph models what I call "Good News for Married Folks." This is timely because many people are saying that the institution of the family is falling apart. I recently attended a conference where we were dealing with a thirty-year-old grandmother. Six months earlier her fourteen-year-old daughter had given birth to a son who will grow up in a house with no positive, black male role models. Over a half million black men are in prison. A recent journal on pastoral care reported that 50 percent of all first marriages end in divorce, 64 percent of all second marriages end in divorce, and 76 percent of all third marriages end in divorce.

With so many people saying that the institution of the family is falling apart, Joseph leaps off of these pages as a man who models good news for married folks. I wish I could count the conversations I have had with church members and friends and other ministers and students about marriages like my parents' as compared with most marriages we see today. My parents are in that 50 percent who never divorced, who never even *talked* about divorce. We know so many divorcees that we tend to forget that there is another 50 percent who have stayed married, happily. My parents have been married fifty-seven years, and a lot of younger folks are wondering, "How is it that they can make it and we can't?" Several young women I know have one eye on that biological clock and another eye on that chronological clock, and a wary and weary eye out on the horizon for a brother who's got something on the ball, hopefully something in the bank, and prayerfully something on his mind other than sex, and they're getting tired of waiting. Some have given up; others are about to give up. You get tired of being lonely. When you become lonely enough, you start settling for anyone, especially if he's got a j-o-b. How do you move from this position of giving up to a posture of looking up?

Joseph's Primary Relationship Was with God

How do you replicate a Jeremiah, Sr., and a Mary Henderson?[4] I think Joseph gives us some clues. When you read Joseph's biography, one of the first things that impresses you is his unswerving, nonnegotiable relationship with God. When you have that primary relationship straight, other relationships are not as difficult to manage.

But a whole lot of us, unlike Joseph, have not even thought about God until after we are married and the marriage is in trouble—after we have moved from what marriage counselors call the being-in-love stage to the struggle-for-power (control) stage. "Who's going to be in charge here? Who has ultimate control in this relationship? I'm a man. I've got to make more money than you, and I'll tell you what you spend and what you don't spend."

The wife says, "Okay, Mr. Macho. You talk all the smack you want, but I've got the keys to the kitchen and to the bedroom." He says, "Hey, ain't no thing. I got a girl down in the valley and another one on the hill, and when I want some lovin', if my valley don't act right, I know my hill will . . . You get my drift?" Power. Control. The sister fires back, "Yeah, well you make sure you stay on out there with your hill, 'cause Mother will kill."

The struggle is for power and control. When we stop being in Luther Vandross love, Anita Baker or Patti LaBelle love, Gladys Knight love, "Do It to Me" Lionel Ritchie love, and get into that next stage of the struggle for power or control, that's when some folks think about God. But if, like Joseph, we have the God relationship straight before we start talking about a marriage relationship, the marriage relationship is not as difficult to manage.

Marriage Is Not Easy

One of the lessons that Joseph teaches us as he brings good news for marriage is that marriage is not easy. The clue to what Joseph is saying is in the names he gives his boys. Look at the first son's name: Manasseh ("God has made me forget all my sufferings").[5] Marriage is hard work. One of the least-liked truths that married couples have to face—and we men have a real problem with this one—is that you don't win all the time. You aren't right all the time, and it isn't going to be your way all the time. One of our elderly deacons summed it up for me many years ago. He and his wife were discussing an issue, and he said, "Rev, she thinks she's always right because of her education and her degrees, and I ain't never right because I don't have no degree. But I happen to know that even a clock that don't work is right twice a day."

You aren't right all the time. You don't win all the time, and it isn't gonna be your way all the time. That's the part of marriage that Paul was referring to when he wrote, "Submit yourselves to one another."[6] You must have some give-and-take. You need to find ways to compromise. You give in sometimes, and she gives in sometimes. You give in sometimes, and he gives in sometimes. Narcissism—my, me, mine—starts to melt into a "we," "our," and "us," and that isn't easy, especially with the philosophies we carry around. You know the philosophies: "Mother is always going to keep her some 'mad' money stashed away, honey." "Girl, always keep you one credit card clear." "Don't be no fool, 'bro; women will take you to the cleaners."

Dr. Samuel Proctor[7] said that if he hadn't had his relationship with Jesus straight and heard Jesus say, "Turn the other cheek"; heard Jesus say, "If you forgive others, I'll forgive you"; heard Jesus say, "Be not overcome with evil, but overcome evil with good"; heard Jesus say, "Vengeance is mine, I will repay"—if he hadn't heard the ethical norms from the voice of his Savior during forty-plus years of marriage, he would have been headed for the divorce lawyer every other week. Marriage is hard work.

I heard an old preacher get in trouble with the sisters at a conference when he started quoting that old chauvinistic line and basing it on Genesis.[8] This old preacher said Adam didn't have any problems while he was all by himself. The sisters started getting quiet. The brother wouldn't stop. He said, "Wasn't no tension. Wasn't no disagreement. Wasn't no disappointment. Wasn't no disillusionment. Wasn't no disobedience. As long as he was by himself, there were no problems. Only when women were created and they were put together were there problems." The sisters were getting quieter and quieter and madder and madder. Then one brother hollered out, "Yeah! He didn't have no problems, but he ain't had no pleasure, either—hallelujah!"

Marriage is both pleasure and problems. Marriage is hard work. It does bring hardship and suffering. Manasseh means "God has made me forget all my sufferings." The good news for married folks is that God will fix it if you keep God central in your situation. God will make you forget all your sufferings.

Marriage Requires Hard Work

But then, look at what else Joseph teaches us. Look at the second son's name: Ephraim ("God has given me children in the land of my trouble").[9] After all that time married to a black fox, married to an African queen, married to a preacher's daughter (her daddy was a priest in Sun City[10]; she knew sacred secrets and she knew sensuous secrets), he was number two in the government, had his own Benz to ride in, and Pharaoh gave him Air Force Two to get around in; he had fine clothes on his back, gold on his neck and fingers, and authority and prosperity[11] —after all that time Joseph still had trouble. Marriage is nonstop work. The trouble doesn't stop the longer you stay married. It does not matter what you achieve on the outside of your home—Mr. Government Official, Mr. Supreme Court Judge, Mr. CEO, Mr. Preacher—you still have to work at home, and sometimes trouble is going to meet you there. Marriage is nonstop work.

But if you look at Joseph, you'll see that God is still kept central in the midst of trouble and in spite of trouble. You don't give up on God because things aren't going the way you wanted them to go. If Joseph's life teaches us anything, it is that it is not about how he started out. He was doomed to fail if his origination was any measure of his destination. It's not about how he started out; it's about how he kept at it. Say to yourself, "I want the Lord to help me keep at it."

His life also teaches us that it is not about what you look like on the outside; it's all about what you look like on the inside. Say to yourself, "I want to look pretty on the inside." His life teaches us that anything worthwhile requires work. Anything worthwhile takes time. There's somebody bigger than the two of you. He said, "God has given me children in the land of my trouble." Joseph brings some good news for married folks—and for my friends who aren't married, too. You don't give up on the ideal, no matter how different or how difficult your situation is as compared to the ideal. You walk on by faith. Have you stumbled and fallen? Get up and walk on by faith.

Trouble Is Real, But So Is God

Faith is the victory. God is with you through your suffering; God is with you in your land of trouble. Is your situation troublesome and not looking anything like Joseph's? Get up! Walk on by faith. I have one friend who told me that it gets lonely, I mean *really* lonely. You are overwhelmed by not having that special, certain someone in your corner who is there no matter what. Well, when it gets like that, don't give up. Get up and walk on by faith. The problems are real, but God is just as real, and he knows all about the problem.

My good friend Dr. Walter Thomas,[12] preaching at the Hampton Ministers Conference,[13] said that in cases like this, you've got to rebuke your revelation. When it has been revealed to you that you are lonely and that you might be alone (and some folks are married and lonely), rebuke that revelation. All revelations are not of God. The devil will show you some things about yourself to have you walking around with your head hung down and feeling bad and down on yourself. You don't believe me? Think about how the devil reveals to you all of your weaknesses and all of your failings, stuff that you have messed up and stuff that you don't want anybody to know. The devil shows it to you. God has forgiven it already, but the devil wants you to see it, dwell on it, and wallow in it. Think about how the devil reveals to you the "should have," "could have," "would have," and "if only," looking at your failed marriage; "if only," looking at your failed relationship; "if only," looking at your child on drugs; and looking at where you are now as opposed to where you could have been. You've got to rebuke that revelation. Say, "Satan, you're a liar."

Rally Your Resources

You've got to rally your resources, and you've got some resources to rally. Faith is one of your resources. "Faith is the substance of things hoped for, the evidence of things not seen."[14] You say, "No, my twenty-five-year marriage didn't make it, but I'm going to walk on by faith." "The just shall live by faith."[15] You not only have faith; you also have prayer as a resource. You have not only you talking to God in prayer—we do too much of that—but also God talking to you in prayer. Listen to him tell you, "You're mine. I made you. I saved you. I redeemed you." "I am the resurrection and the life."[16] "I am the root of Jesse."[17] "I am the good shepherd."[18] "I am the way, the truth, and the life."[19] "I am bread when you're hungry; I am water when you're thirsty; I am your bridge over troubled water. I am a friend when you don't have one." Yes, your problems are real, but God is just as real. God says, "I am the problem solver."

There are some things I may not know, some places I may not go. But this one thing I know for sure: when you let God talk to you, he'll tell you, "Oh, yes. I'm real." He'll put a little fire down on the inside and start something to turning. Sometimes when you're all by yourself, you may be *alone*, but you're not *lonely* because you can feel him deep within, moving on the inside. And with God on the inside, things start getting better on the outside. No, things haven't changed in terms of your location, but your situation gets better when you start focusing on God and taking the focus off of yourself.

Devotional

Songs of Praise
Prayer
Scripture: Genesis 41:45-52
Song: "Yes, God Is Real"

Study Questions

1. By contemporary standards, Joseph's family of birth would be considered dysfunctional. What happened in his family? In addition, his young adult life was marred by betrayal and imprisonment. How was he betrayed, and why was he imprisoned?

2. What were Joseph's genealogical, physiological, and sociological circumstances? What are similar circumstances that young men, and particularly African American men, face today?

3. Why didn't Joseph's circumstances "circumscribe his possibilities"?

4. What Scriptures are mentioned in this sermon that can be used to form a theology for overcoming negative circumstances? What other Scriptures, doctrines of the church, or folk wisdom might be used?

5. What is the connection between having one's primary relationship with God in order and achieving stability in one's family life?

6. The elderly deacon at Trinity Church talks about having a wife who has to be right all of the time. Another scenario in the sermon demonstrates one-upmanship in marital power plays. Role-play these two scenes with at least one partner, allowing yourself to be led by God's Spirit and applying the biblical principles that Dr. Proctor mentions.

7. What are some other ways that married couples vie for power? What spiritual and biblical principles and Christlike behaviors can be applied to overcome this negative behavior?

8. The names of Joseph's sons—"God has made me forget all my sufferings" (Manasseh) and "God has given me children in the land

of my trouble" (Ephraim)—are cited as characteristics of marriage. These names indicate that marriage imparts rich blessings, but they are also reminders that marriage is not easy and that it requires hard work. Name some blessings in marriage that must be maintained by hard work. What happens in marriage when we take our blessings for granted?

9. "Rebuking a revelation" does not mean denying the truth of an event in your life. What does it mean, and how would you go about exercising this spiritual weapon?

10. Practice listening to the revelations of God as an added dimension to your prayer life. Hear God's affirmations of you and God's promises to you. Allow these to be antidotes to the devil's negative and accusatory revelations against you.

Good News for Single Folks

Luke 15:11-32

Introduction

Terry McMillan's book *Waiting to Exhale* gives some in-depth glimpses of four black women: Savannah, Bernadine, Robin, and Gloria.[1] All of them are in their middle to late thirties, single, and searching for happiness. As McMillan carries you through the various changes in their lives, she skillfully, masterfully, powerfully, and artistically draws a composite sketch of what it means to be black, single, and searching—something with which a lot of us can identify.

When I announced that I would be preaching on "Good News for Single Folks" at Trinity,[2] one of our sisters hollered out, "Thank you!" That's because so many churches operate as if single people were either nonexistent or superhuman. Much of church planning and programming is done with either intentional slights or thoughtless and unintentional slaps: the family nights that actually are for married folks or the couples clubs that ignore the fact that everybody isn't part of a couple.

Likewise, the sermons and Bible classes are designed for a superhuman who is a nonsexual person living in a sex-saturated culture. That's a nonexistent person. Let's establish four points. First, 50 percent of all marriages end in divorce. That means 50 percent of all people who tried marriage ended up single again. God's got some good news for you. Second, there are three kinds of singles in our society: those who have never been married, those who have been married and are now divorced, and those who are widows and widowers. God has some good news for you. Third, if all of the single people eighteen years old and above in almost any church service were asked to stand, a large percentage of the congregation would be standing. God has some good news for all these folks who love the Lord and who are ignored by preachers all over this land. Fourth, do you know the whole range of feelings that married people have? Single people have those same feelings. What runs through a married person's mind also runs through a single person's mind. Single people have needs and hungers like married people do.

Two illustrations bring this point to life: First, several years ago at a church retreat, one of the members pulled me out of the lunch line and said, "Reverend, I've got to talk to you right now!" It was urgent. "We can sit right here," I replied. "No," she said, "Not in here. I don't want anybody to hear this." I put my tray down, and we went outside. She said, "Tell me, is God going to send me to hell if I'm not celibate until I get married again? That's what the folk in my group are saying. Talk to me, Pastor." Single people have needs and hungers like married people do.

Second, our church conducted a seminar on "Sex and the Single Christian." The single-adult minister came to me and we planned it, thinking we might generate some interest. The seminar was to run for four weeks, with a format of one hour for the lecture, thirty minutes for questions and answers, and thirty minutes for socializing. The singles had about fifteen active members, and they thought they would double their membership by offering this seminar.

The first night of the scheduled seminar, the custodian came to my office while members of the single-adult ministry and I were photocopying material to hand out on sex in the Bible and Christians and contemporary thinking about sex. The custodian said, "Reverend, where do you want to put these folk?" I said, "What folk?" He said, "The folk who are coming to this 'Sex and the Single Christian' seminar." I said, "Right out here in the fellowship hall. Where else can we have a social hour?" He said, "I don't think there's gonna be no social hour here tonight. You got over four hundred people out there waiting to hear this topic."

There is no nonsexual person living today in our sex-saturated culture. One sister hollered out, "Thank you!" because she was tired of churches acting as though singles were nonexistent and most of all because she wanted to know, "Is there any word from the Lord?"[3]

Is There Any Word from the Lord?

Terry McMillan's character Gloria is the only one of the four who wants to know that same thing: "Is there any word from the Lord?" Over and over as a pastor, I am asked, "Is there any word from the Lord?" If you are a single black man with a job, people think something must be wrong with you if you don't have a wife and you're thirty-something. Is there any word from the Lord? If you're a black man without a job, forget it; you ain't even in the running. I don't care what you've got going for you in terms of character. Is there any word from the Lord? If you're not in the networking loop, the black buppie loop, the young professional set, or the college-trained, BMW-driving, condo-owning, Martel-drinking, say-no-to-cocaine-now-that-I'm-a-little-older clique, you are defective. Is there any word from the Lord?

If you are a single black woman, you're damned if you do and damned if you don't. I remember one of the best arguments we had during that seminar. I was busy describing black men who are committed to women and God, not men who use or abuse women, treating them as nonpersons or objects. After I finished, a sister asked, "Where are you going to find a brother like that?" All the sisters said, "Right on, girl. If you don't get up off it, they are going to leave you, and if you do, you ain't the marrying kind." The sisters said, "Right on, girl." Then a brother stood up and said, "You're right, sister, absolutely right. And you know who taught me to be like this? My mama. I was raised by a woman. Y'all made us this way." The rest of that night's seminar turned into a male-female argument!

If you're a woman, single, and black, you're damned if you do and damned if you don't. If you're pretty, educated, and articulate, you are a threat to the notion of macho manhood and an assault upon many males' fragile egos. If you are professional and articulate, then don't fall for the hype that says you must be a lesbian. If you are a single parent, divorced, and have some responsibility on your mind, you can forget it. The brothers aren't interested. Married sisters don't want you around their men; the church mothers are trying to marry you off to anybody with breath and britches, and your own mother is worrying you to death about finding "Mr. Right." One of my single brothers told me that his mother has gotten to the point where she says, "Now baby, that one didn't drool while she ate, and she has all her parts. What's wrong with her?"

We know what the word is from our parents; we know what the word is from our married friends—and some of our married friends are in the category of misery loving company. We know what the word is from our experienced friends; we know what the word is from our gay friends, our saved friends, and our make-pretend-they're-saved friends, but what we want to know is, "Is there any word from the Lord?"

God Welcomes Outsiders

What does God have to say to those who are single, whom the church considers nonexistent outsiders and unwanted? In the story that Jesus tells in Luke 15, the first bit of good news is this: those whom the righteous consider outsiders God welcomes in. Both the context and content of this story reinforce that truth. Consider the context. In verse 1, the Word says, "One time many tax collectors and outcasts came to listen to Jesus." They came to listen because they knew the Lord of the church had a word for them even if the church did not. When they came, the righteous, the saints, the saved-and-sanctified folk had a fit. The Pharisees and the teachers of the law started grumbling, "This man welcomes outcasts and even eats with them!" (v. 2). That is the context in which this story is told. When he heard them grumbling, Jesus told three stories that are recorded in this chapter: one about a lost sheep, one about a lost coin, and one about a lost son. Those whom the righteous consider outsiders, outcasts, God welcomes in.

Now look at the content. The younger son knew he would be viewed by the insiders as someone defective. That is why he said, "I am no longer fit to be called your son; treat me as one of your hired workers" (v. 19)—an outsider. The older brother was so angry that he would not greet his brother. He put himself out of the family. One of the most pitiful practices that I saw when I was growing up was the Victorian, Puritan, Scarlet-Letter[4] mentality that made unmarried girls who became pregnant get up in front of the church and confess that they had sinned. They were outsiders, outcasts, unfit to be a part of the body of Christ. I felt that that was barbaric and unkind! They never made the men stand up and confess. Nor did they make the wife beater stand up and confess. Nor did they make the incestuous slime stand up and confess. Nor did they make dirty deacons and tricky trustees stand up and confess. We had this holier-than-thou mentality that said, "They got what they deserve. Their actions have put them beyond the pale of the Christian community. They're outsiders."

But thank God, those whom the righteous consider outsiders, the Father welcomes in. "Go, kill the fatted calf! Come on, let's celebrate and have a feast! Bring the best robe and put it on him. Put a ring on his finger. And bring some Bruno Maglis for his feet." Those whom the righteous try to keep out, God welcomes in. This story teaches us that those whom the righteous can't stand to be around, God can't stand to be without. The older brother, like a lot of church folk, didn't even want to be in the same room with the wrongdoer. Verse 28 says that the older brother was so angry that he didn't even want to go into the house. But while he was being so perfect and so self-righteous, look at what God was doing (v. 20): The father (who symbolizes God) was gazing out toward the horizon daily, waiting, hoping, and looking for some sign of his wayward child. The father couldn't stand to be without him. One of our hymn writers captured the power of that verse when he wrote, "Softly and tenderly Jesus is calling, calling for you and for me. See, on the portals he's waiting and watching, watching for you and for me. Come home, come home, ye who are weary, come home."[5]

I often recall the disk jockey from Philadelphia, where I grew up, who used to sign off the air each night with these words: "If you don't feel as close to God as you once did, remember which one of you did the straying." The son did the straying. The son walked off and left his father. We as God's children pull away from what we once had, but the Father scans the horizon day after day, looking, watching, and hoping for us to come back home. He can't stand to be without us. The text says that when he saw him from a long way off (you can recognize somebody you love from a long way off, no matter how badly beaten down or how raggedy or barefoot that loved one is) the father knew that was his child. When he saw him a long way off, he ran. He couldn't stand to be without him. He did not stroll casually; he did not meander nonchalantly; he did not say, "I'll teach this boy a lesson." He ran, threw his arms around him, and kissed his son. Those whom the righteous can't stand to be around, God can't stand to be without.

This story also teaches us something about those whom the righteous hate, talk about, and tell on. Let's look at the righteous. In the first place, they're grumbling because they don't like the folk that Jesus likes. Some of us don't want Jesus to like the folk that we don't like. In verse 2, they're talking about the folk that Jesus is with. In verses 29 and 30, the righteous brother is telling on his baby brother. "He disobeyed your orders; I didn't. You're giving him something; you didn't give me anything. He wasted all your property. He has been with prostitutes." Notice that the baby boy didn't tell his daddy that. Mr. Self-Righteous had to tell him. Isn't it curious how the righteous feel they always have to tell on other folks and tell God what somebody else is doing? In Luke 18:11-12, the righteous Pharisee is telling on folks in his prayer: "I thank you, God, that I am not like everybody else. Everybody else is doing wrong, but I'm in the clear. I thank you that I'm not like that tax collector over there." The self-righteous always feel they've got to tell on others and talk about others. But Jesus says those whom the righteous hate, talk about, and tell on are loved by God unconditionally. God doesn't put conditions on his love like we put on our love.

Our Relationship with God Determines How We Relate to Others

Beyond the obvious lessons in this story, God showed me as I prayed over this passage something else that I want you to see. What God showed me is that the relationship we have with him is the prerequisite for what happens in our other relationships. The relationships we have with other people all are predicated upon our relationship with him. It has become clear to me that one of the reasons we have so many problems is that we are in the church but we are not in relationship with the Lord. We are in different ministries, but we're not in relationship with the Lord.

Our young people are being pulled away from the church by various sects and cults because they have no relationship with the Lord. When I was in Detroit for the annual Conference on African American Male Spirituality, I was talking about brothers having their relationship with the Lord straight before having a relationship with a sister. In the question-and-answer period, they mentioned that the Nation of Islam is doing a lot of recruiting and suggested that, as a Christian minister, I might be jealous of the Nation. I'm not jealous; I'm just worried about the brothers who don't have a relationship with the Lord. If the gangs come after you, the average Christian isn't going to do anything but pray for you. But if you put on a bow tie and say, "As *salaam alaikum*,"[6] the gangs are going to leave you alone because they don't mess with the Fruit of Islam.[7] Which would you choose?

But the problem is not about "As *salaam alaikum*," not about the Qur'an,[8] because half of the brothers haven't read the Qur'an. It's about your relationship with Jesus Christ. The question that was asked of Peter was, "Who do *you* say I am?" (Matthew 16:15). He didn't ask him who Muhammad said he was or who Elijah said he was. He said, "Who do *you* say I am?" That's the relationship question. After I finished talking, a brother stood up at that Detroit meeting and said, "My pastor, my brother, my friend, you don't know me, but I want to affirm every word you have just said. I was a practicing Muslim for twenty-five years, but I'd only *heard* about Jesus. Now that I've *met* the Lord, I'm saved and sanctified and in the church of Jesus Christ because I have a relationship with him."

The older brother in the parable had a dysfunctional relationship with his father. He didn't do what he did based on love and grace, gratitude and glory. He was operating on a quid pro quo[9] basis, a tit-for-tat basis: "I'll do this for you if you do that for me." This is the same way many of us treat God: "I've worked for you like a slave, and you haven't given me a party." His relationship with his father distorted his relationship with his brothers and sisters. Because he and the father didn't have the right kind of relationship, he could not be in a healthy relationship with his own brother. That's the negative side of this relationship issue.

Let's look at the positive side. When your relationship with God is straight, other relationships will take care of themselves. Look at verses 17 through 19. That's when the boy came to himself. That's when he came to his senses. That's when he realized that his relationship with his father was not what it should have been. He said, "I will get up and go to my father and say, 'Father, I have sinned against God and against you. I am no longer fit to be called your son'" (vv. 18-19). It's an issue of relationship. So he got up and started back to his father. One of our church hymns says, "Coming home, coming home, nevermore to roam. Open now thine arms of love—Lord, I'm coming home."[10] When you get your relationship with God straight, all of the other relationships start taking care of themselves.

First, there will be some who like you. In verse 25, there is music and dancing. Please note: this isn't church music being played. They're not having a worship service. They're dancing at a party. That's in the Bible. Jesus said it was a party. It's in the Book—music and dancing. I was hanging out with some Church of God in Christ folk, and they put this dancing thing in perspective for me. Yes, I used to dance in the world. Guess what? I'm in the church now; I've just changed partners! Some folk will rejoice with you and your relationship with God. Some will enjoy being in your company and having a good time. Some will be happy just because you're happy. Some will enjoy partying with you just because you are you. They will love you for who you are, not for what you pretend to be. Everybody at that party knew that this boy had blown it, but they did not like or dislike him on the basis of his performance; they liked him on the basis of his personhood. There will be some who will like you.

Second, there will be some, like his older brother, who will never like you. But it's all right. Please notice that the party doesn't stop because the older brother is upset. No, no! Don't let other folk who have a problem make their problem your problem. Don't you slow down because some evil person wants to pull you down. You put your hand in God's hand and keep on stepping. Some of them won't ever like you. You get your relationship with God straight, and some are going to like you just because you're you, and some will never like you. But then, once your relationship with the Father is straight, who likes you and who doesn't like you is no longer an issue. Who you are and *whose* you are—"I'm his and he's mine. I'm a child of the King"— will be the only issue. You'll find yourself walking around singing crazy songs like, "If anybody asks you who I am, who I am, who I am, if anybody asks you who I am, tell them I'm a child of God."[11]

You see, who you are and whose you are changes how you feel. It changes how you act; it changes where you go. It changes what you do; it changes what you will put up with and what you don't have to take anymore. Who you are and whose you are determines what you settle for and who you go out with. Who you are and whose you are puts you at peace with yourself, and it stops that frantic thirst for wholeness that can never be quenched by another human person—and makes whatever God sends your way that day all right with you. Who you are and whose you are starts you off in a different place. You start with loving the Lord, and you're not ashamed to tell anybody, "I love the Lord. You don't know what he's done for me. He welcomed me in. He keeps his loving arms around me. He keeps doing great things for me. He's making a way for me, and makes me feel like no woman or no man can make me feel."

Can't nobody treat you like Jesus. Who you are and whose you are will allow you to make it all right with whatever God sends your way that day. I really love the Lord. Do you love the Lord? You don't know what he's done for me. He gave me the victory! I really love the Lord.

Devotional

Songs of Praise
Prayer
Scripture: Luke 15:11-32
Song: "I Really Love the Lord"

Study Questions

1. How would you answer the question that was posed by the single woman: "Is God going to send me to hell if I'm not celibate until I get married again?" What advice would you give to her?

2. In what ways can popular culture in the United States be considered sex-saturated?

3. It has often been said that mothers rear their daughters but spoil their sons. In the sermon text, a young man is quoted as saying that his upbringing by his mother contributed to his negative behavior toward women. Is there any validity to this statement? If so, can you identify any child-rearing practices and teachings of mothers (past and present) that might be detrimental to their sons' future relationships with women? What about positive teachings and practices that would be beneficial to their sons' future relationships with women?

4. Are you the mother of a son? Are you rearing him so that he will be a desirable and responsible mate when he becomes an adult?

5. Conduct a special Bible study that includes a profile of Terry McMillan's four women characters in *Waiting to Exhale*. Discuss their experiences and points of view. What can they do to improve their situations? What "word from the Lord" would you offer in ministry to each of them?

6. How are singles treated in your church or organization? Is there room for improvement? What improvements would you suggest?

7. Who are the outsiders in your church, organization, or group?

What are some of the prevailing attitudes toward them? How do these attitudes reflect a self-righteous spirit?

8. Role-play a situation that demonstrates the group's feelings toward outsiders. Let someone be the bearer of God's Spirit. What would that person say to or do with the insiders? What would he or she say to or do with the outsiders?

9. How can one form a relationship with God?

10. How does the relationship with God straighten out other relationships? How does it satisfy a person so that he or she "can make it all right with whatever God sends that day"? What sorts of things does God send that sustain us?

Good News for Good Parents

Matthew 4:21-22; 20:20-22

Introduction

We hear so much news about bad parents. We hear so many instances of bad parenting and poor choices made by parents. We hear so many people hiding behind the cop-out "Well, I ain't never been a parent before," as if that exonerates them somehow from the criticism they so richly deserve for some poor decisions they have made. We are always hearing about bad parents: absentee daddies and abusive mommies, daddies who drink too much and mommies who work too much, daddies with two or three chicks on the side and mommies with "cousins" who keep saying, "You can't miss what you can't measure."[1] We're always hearing about bad parents who had no time for their children, who kept the streets hot and let love die; parents who robbed their children of their heritage and history and kept their children away from their grandparents; parents who robbed their children of a religious upbringing; parents who confused their children by saying one thing and doing another, promising one thing and never delivering on their promises. Then there's confused parenting: they were Baptists when the child was born, Nationalists when the child was weaned, Seventh Day Adventists when the child started school, Muslims when the child finished school, Jehovah's Witnesses when the child got married, and followers of the Temple of Kemet when their grandchild was born. Completely messed up.

We are always hearing horror story after horror story about bad parents, sexually abusive parents, spouse-abusing parents, substance-abusing parents, parents who were kids when they had kids and now that their kids are grown up, they're still kids—grown kids—trying to look younger, act younger, dress younger, date younger, and sleep younger than their own grown kids. We are always hearing so much about the bad parents that we ignore God's word for those who are trying to be good parents.

I see Val and Ethel Jordan, who raised all of their children in the church. They didn't send them; they brought them. Good parents. I see Mike and Cheryl Brown. I see Michael and Carol Jacobs.[2] They are *with* their children in church every Sunday. Good parents. I see my mama and my daddy, who helped us with homework and taught us to do housework; who took us to Sunday school and BTU;[3] who took the time to teach us the Word of God at home; who introduced us to the Lord and showed us how to pray; who proved to us that when you call on the Lord you will get an answer; who drilled into us that God cares, God hears, God can, and God is. Good parents.

I also see many single parents who are good parents. I see Pierre, a single daddy, raising his family in the fear and admonition of the Lord. I see Elizabeth and Brenda, Janet and Jeri. I see Denise and Leslie[4]—fathers and mothers who have learned how to trust the Lord and take him at his word. Good parents. These folk may not have a mate, but they have a firm hand in the Master's hand, and they are determined to mold and shape their children in the image of Christ. Good parents. I see so many good parents, some of whom were bad wives and bad husbands, but who have combined their efforts, stood shoulder to shoulder, walked together, pooled their resources, and raised their children as best they could so that the children understood that the divorce was between the parents and not between parent and child. Many parents have done and are doing a good job.

I've seen so many good parents that I began to search the Scriptures to see what paradigms were lifted up and what word God had for good parents. In the Scripture I found a portrait of two good parents: Zebedee and Salome, parents of James and John. James and John are brothers in the faith who are strong, rough men. Their reputation in Holy Writ is that of prophets of doom who will not take any stuff. Mark 9 records an incident that they had with a brother whom they "jacked up" to such an extent that he was afraid to mention the name of Jesus.[5] These were some rough brothers. When a Samaritan village refused hospitality to their friend and leader, these two brothers wanted to call down lightning and fire somebody up for such a thoughtless and disrespectful act: "You must not know who our Jesus is, talking about you don't want him in your town. We will kick your butt and take your name. We're fired up, and not only are we fired up, we're wired up, and we'll fire you up."[6] These were some rough brothers. They were known as the Brothers Boanerges, the Sons of Thunder.[7] James and John were dedicated, serious, and sincere—and they were the sons of Zebedee and Salome.

Good Parents Shape Their Children's Character

Zebedee and Salome raised these boys and shaped and molded their character. Zebedee and Salome taught them the value of hard work, an honest day's work. When Jesus walks up on them, they're working with their daddy and know the pride one can feel when one has done a good job. These boys were not ashamed. They were aggressive and assertive because of the way they were raised. They had good parents. The biblical portrait presents good parents who took seriously their responsibility of shaping character.

In our men's Bible class we have studied the importance of the family and the extended family in helping to shape the moral values of boys and girls. We teach our children the importance of church by the way we talk about the church, by the way we tithe to the church, by the way we work in the church. We give our children their values at home, and they get their trimmings at church. They learn honesty at home. They learn integrity at home. They learn respect at home. They learn right from wrong at home. They learn dignity at home. They learn responsibility at home. They learn the importance of God's Word at home. They learn the centrality of prayer at home. As a friend of mine says, "You can't be what you can't see." If they never see you pray at home, then prayer for them becomes either an activity we engage in up at the church or it becomes a hypocritical act we pretend to engage in for the sake of public piety. It is that simple. What they see at home is what shapes their character. Good parents take seriously the responsibility of shaping character. If you shout all over the church and praise God all over the church and get home and run the church down all around the dinner table or on the telephone, your children aren't getting *mixed* signals—they're getting *clear* signals about what you think about the church.

Good Parents Share Their Children's Crises

Good parents not only take seriously the responsibility of shaping character; they take seriously the responsibility of sharing crises. When crises come into our children's lives, we too often brush them aside as unimportant or trivial. So often we do untold damage that will take years to repair. We need to share in our children's crises. I don't mean just the major traumas that can lead to antisocial behavior; I mean crises of identity and crises of personality development. The world tells them something different from what you've been telling them. That creates a crisis. You are trying to raise your child one way, telling your daughter one thing, and then some little hard-legged boy whispers something else in her ear, and all the while the hormones are raging. You've got a crisis in your home. When you are telling your son that this is what it takes to be a man, and his partners are telling him something else (peer pressure is a pistol), you've got a crisis in your home.

Can you remember the crisis moments in your life? Not just in the area of sexuality but also in the area of nationality. When did you learn the negative conceptions concerning the color of your skin? That was a crisis.

I remember a double whammy of self-concept formation. Being impacted by outside perception, I went home for lunch one day in the sixth grade with a Jewish friend of mine, and his mama freaked. She didn't want a *schwartze*[8] in her home. My daddy had to explain to me what a *schwartze* was and why some whites hate us for no reason. My parents shared in my crisis. Then, when my black buddy told me that his mama had told him never to trust yellow people, that caused another crisis. Why was I being judged on the basis of how God made me? I didn't have anything to do with this. Whites don't like you because you're black, and blacks don't like you because you're yellow. My parents had to sit me down and explain to me about slavery and the psychological images held over from slavery, stuff they thought they had left behind in the South. My parents shared in my crises. Good parents take seriously the responsibility of shaping character and the responsibility of sharing crises.

Good Parents Show Christ to Their Children

Good parents also take seriously the responsibility of showing Christ. James and John were raised in Jewish families. Like Andrew and Peter, they knew about Jesus through the message that John preached about the One who was coming. James and John also had heard of One who could speak and give sight to the blind, speak and cause deaf men to hear, speak and calm down angry waves, speak and cause fishermen to leave their nets. They had heard at home of him whom the angels call holy.

What have your children heard at home? My parents demonstrated at home what it meant to be under the lordship of Christ. My daddy tithed. My mother prayed. I will never forget one time when I was so young I still slept in my crib but was old enough to get out of the crib at night and climb into their bed. I would wait until they were sound asleep before making my move. One night in the middle of the night, as I got out of my crib, I found that they were not in their bed. They were on their knees praying, all by themselves. There were no children to imprint, no church folk to impress—just praying by themselves. They showed me with their lives what they professed with their lips. Good parents take seriously the responsibility of showing Christ.

A whole lot of young people are confused about what they hear in the streets, in the schools, or somewhere else because they have not come from homes where they are shown daily the Christ of Calvary. Good parents have a responsibility to shape character, share crises, and show Christ.

Parents Have a Right to Demand Obedience

There is a responsibility factor in being a good parent, as well as a rights factor. We hear a lot of talk about children's rights, but parents have rights, too. Let's examine two of these rights, especially as they are evident in the lives of James and John, Zebedee and Salome's boys.

First, as a parent, you have a right to demand obedience. We have a whole bunch of children who are raising adults these days and adults who are afraid to be adults. You have a right to demand obedience. At the recent United Charities Annual Conference, I was sharing with the conferees a conversation I heard when I called Jawanza Kunjufu's home.[9] I called Jawanza's home but couldn't get him to come to the phone because he was engaged in a heated discussion with his teenage son. So I talked with his wife and tried to hear what his wife was saying amidst all the noise in the background.

The problem was that his son had some rap music that disrespected women, and he wanted to play that in Jawanza's house. And Jawanza said, "Not here. Not in this house." The son countered, "I can hear it on the radio." "You're going to turn from the station if it comes on the radio," Jawanza shot back. "I don't even know why you're listening to that station in the first place." "But I can hear it in the street," his son argued. "I don't pay the rent in the street," said Jawanza, "but I do pay the house note here, and you're not going to play that in this house!" Parents have a right to demand obedience.

I was telling the folks at the conference that we didn't have rap when I was young. We had something called "doo-wop." When I was young, the musicians sang music instead of talking it. But all of our songs weren't that good in terms of content either. We had forty-fives, and they cost less than a dollar. I bought a forty-five RPM[10] called "Cherry Pie."[11] It was a very simple little song. It didn't have a whole lot of words, but it was one of those good "grinding" (slow sensual dancing that was fashionable for teenagers in the fifties) songs. I took it home and began playing it: "Cherry, cherry pie. Cherry, cherry pie. Oooo, so good." The second verse came on: "Gimme, gimme some . . ."

That's as far as the record got before my mama was in my room and taking the needle up off my forty-five. There wasn't any discussion. She broke my forty-five and said, "If I ever catch you playing it in here or listening to it again, I'm going to beat you from an amazing grace to a floating opportunity." Parents have a right to demand obedience.

Parents Have a Right to Demand Uniqueness

Parents also have a right to demand uniqueness. James and John were unique. They did not go along with the crowd. Tell your children that it is all right to be different. They don't have to be carbon copies of their friends. Be unique. When all the boys want to wear their pants halfway down their hips with the belt open and the gym shoes untied and have twenty-seven parts in their heads, platted pony tails down their backs, and an earring in their ear, you be unique. Pull your pants up on your body. Fasten your belt. Tie your shoes. Put on a shirt and tie. Stand up like a man and learn something other than, "Yo, what's up?" Look at Dr. Ben Carson.[12] Look at Martin Luther King, Jr. Look at Malcolm X. Stand up tall, be unique, be different, be you. You're not a clone or a carbon copy of somebody else. You have a right, parent, to demand uniqueness.

Parents Have a Right to Demand Excellence

You have a right to demand excellence. Mediocrity is killing us. Why settle for second best when you can go first-class? Demand excellence of your children. If you give them no goals, they will reach none. Tell them you expect excellence in all that they do. Please notice: Excellence does not mean perfection. We put unnecessary pressure on our children when we push them for perfection. Nobody is perfect, not even you. Don't push for perfection. But you can demand excellence. We did not get to where we are with a that-will-do attitude. We got here because of excellence. Whether it's Willie Taplan Barrow in a pulpit or Mae Jemison in a cockpit, the standard is excellence. Whether it's Arthur Ashe on a tennis court or Michael Jordan on a basketball court or Thurgood Marshall in the Supreme Court, the standard is excellence. Whether Langston Hughes writing or Muhammad Ali fighting, the standard is still excellence. Whether Oprah in the daytime or Arsenio in the nighttime or Ray Charles singing "The Right Time," the standard is still excellence. Whether Vashti McKenzie in the A.M.E. church, Dr. D. Brown Daniels in the Baptist church, Cynthia Hale in the Disciples church, or Johnnie Coleman in the Universal church, the standard is still excellence. Whether Wynton Marsalis on trumpet, Kirk Whalum on saxophone, Stevie Wonder behind the keyboard, or Ozzie Smith behind the pulpit, the standard is still excellence. Whether Cheikh Anta Diop in history, Zora Neale Hurston in folklore, Sterling Brown in literature, Terry McMillan in fiction, Spike Lee in films, Paula Giddings in journalism, Ivan Van Sertima in anthropology, James Cone and John Kinney in theology, the standard is still excellence.[13]

As a parent, you have a right to demand obedience. There are rules in this house. You have a right to demand uniqueness, and you have a right to demand excellence. There are some rights that you can and must exercise as a parent. Good parents demand obedience, uniqueness, and excellence.

Good Parents Lay a Religious Foundation for Their Children

Good parents don't leave the religious foundation in their children's lives up to chance: what they *might* hear in church, what they *might* hear in school, or what they *might* hear on the street. Good parents lay that foundation themselves the way Zebedee and Salome did.

Good parents teach the Bible. If you don't want some Five Percenters[14] incorrectly teaching the pieces of the Qur'an they've appropriated for themselves, you'd better teach the Bible at home. If you don't want some Jehovah's Witnesses confusing your kids with a verse from over here and a word from over there, you'd better teach your child the Bible at home. Make Bible reading as fundamental as breakfast eating; you don't do one without the other. Of course, I know that raises a problem, because you can't teach what you don't know. Good parents know and teach the Bible.

Good parents also teach prayer. Teach your children to pray. You don't have anything to be ashamed of. Prayer changes things. Prayer is holy communication. Prayer is the key to heaven. Prayer is hooking up with the holy. Prayer changes people. Prayer opens you up so that God can get in and sweep out. Teach your children to pray. Other folk may be embarrassed about the privacy of prayer. You teach them to call him in the morning, call him in the noon hour, call him when the sun goes down. "Jesus is on the main line. Tell him what you want." You don't want somebody else to teach your children prayer. You teach them. Good parents teach the Word. Good parents teach prayer.

Good Parents Teach Children Their History

Good parents also teach history. James and John were not confused about who they were. They knew their history and God's mighty acts in their history just as well as they knew their names. They knew his presence, and they knew his promises. They were able to drop their nets and follow Jesus because they knew their history. They also knew their destiny. That's why they followed so faithfully.

Don't be ashamed of your history. Teach your children our history. Tell them how God used to meet us in the cane breaks and commune with us in the brush arbors. Tell them how God made a way out of no way; tell them what God did for our folks who were brutalized and dehumanized. Teach your children our history. Don't think someone else is going to teach them. Our history is a central piece of our religious experience.

Some of us get confused. We want to divorce our race from our religion. We want to teach doctrine as separate and distinct from the raw data of our racist existence in this strange land. You can't do it. Our history is an indispensable part of our religious heritage. The African *did* live through the hell of slavery and come through singing "How I Got Over." The Africans *were* mistreated by white Christians who wore black robes by day and white robes by night, but they held on anyhow to God's unchanging hand because they knew of a God who sat higher than slavery and who made them in his own image. The Africans created the spirituals and gave us our common-meter songs.[15] Teach your children our history.

Half of our children couldn't answer if you were to start off singing, "I, I, I love the Lord. He heard my cry."[16] You've got to *teach* that. They aren't going to learn that in any music class or private academy, but it's a part of who we are. Long before slavery, the Africans knew the Lord. In fact, he was African too. Teach that part of your history. Good parents teach the Bible. They teach our history.

Good Parents Teach the Faith

Salome wanted her boys to have the best because she had raised them in the faith. Teach our children, "If you're going to eat Mama's greens, then you're going to serve Mama's God." That's a paraphrase of my favorite line from Lorraine Hansberry's play *A Raisin in the Sun*. Beneatha came home "conscious."[17] She'd become a nationalist. She didn't believe in God anymore. She was discarding all of her Christian baggage. She had an African boyfriend, Asagai, whose name she tried to teach her mother to pronounce. Her mama said to her—her mama who had called on the Lord and scrimped and saved long before Beneatha could pronounce her own name, much less her boyfriend's African name—her mama said, "In this house, there is still God."

Teach the faith. It's "the substance of things hoped for, the evidence of things not seen."[18] Teach them, "The LORD is my light and my salvation."[19] Teach them, "God is my refuge and strength."[20] God is the joy and the strength of my life. God is a rock in a weary land, a shelter in the time of storm. God is a body healer and mind regulator, and God is good all the time. Teach them our faith. There's nothing wrong in loving the Lord. If the Lord has been good to you, then you ought to tell somebody. If the Lord has made a way for you, then you ought to tell somebody. If the Lord woke you up this morning, if he started you on your way, say, "Lord I love you. I love you, Lord." Don't be ashamed of the Lord.

Devotional

Songs of Praise
Prayer
Scripture: Matthew 4:21-22; 20:20-22
Song: "The Lord Is Blessing Me Right Now"

Study Questions

1. What is one of the most important things parents can do to shape their children's character?

2. Why is the home more important as the central place for learning values than either the church or school?

3. What kinds of crises in identity and personality development do African American children face?

4. In what ways can parents share their children's crises?

5. James and John eagerly followed Jesus. Reread Matthew 4:21-22 and 20:20-22. What indications are in these texts that Zebedee and Salome prepared James and John for Jesus' coming?

6. What parenting style(s) will best allow parents to demand obedience of their children? Choose one or more of the following styles and elaborate:

a. Friendship style: The child and the parent are "buddies."

b. Authoritarian style: The parent is the sole authority and is not to be questioned.

c. Leadership style: The parent is the adult leader in the family and is invested with maturity, wisdom, and the power to make decisions.

7. Peer pressure and the search for personal identity cause children and teens to want to conform to what their friends are doing. Given these realities, how can parents encourage "uniqueness" when their children are saying, "But everybody's doing it. Why can't I?"

8. How can parents demand excellence of their children without seeming to demand perfection?

9. Who are some good parents you know? Share their positive parenting qualities with the group.

10. What resources can parents use to help themselves educate their children about religious faith? What resources can help them teach their children their history?

Good News for Blended Families

Luke 2:41-52

Introduction

A few years ago, one of my deacons asked me during "Family Month" at Trinity to bring the Word of God to the intersection where he lived. "What does God have to say," he asked me, "about blended families?" These are families in which there are children by some other union. What does the Word of God have to say about blended families?

When it comes to the contemplation of marriage into such a family, I know what people say. I've seen people afraid of building a relationship because of what somebody else has said. A daddy with a mind by Mattel will tell his son, "You don't want to marry into that instant family. Now you think real hard before you do something foolish. She already has a baby by somebody else."

This demonstrates the victimization and further alienation of a woman who has already been messed over by one boy and is now being forsaken or passed over by another boy who can't think for himself but, like Oedipus,[1] has to work out or work through some unresolved issues with his daddy. His daddy says, "You don't want to marry a woman who already has children," and he listens not to his full heart but to his empty-headed daddy who thinks that a woman with children is all right to sleep with but not to build a life with. "You can make love *to* them, but you can't make a life *with* them." This is what I mean by "a mind by Mattel." These are people who think women are toys to be played with but not persons with whom to share life.

I know what people say about marriage into such a family. Some women feel that if the first relationship doesn't work out, they are doomed to a long list of transient friends who come in and out of their lives or who say that they are committed, and stay committed to being friends, but frown on being husbands. I know what people say about those families where there is a child or children from some other union. I know what people say when it comes to contemplating marriage into such a family. But what does the Lord say? Is there any word from the Lord?

A Home Where God Is Honored

I submit to you that not only does God have a lot to say on this subject of blended families, but that among the first things God says is, "Yes, I understand because my Son was part of such a family. I have a whole lot to say about such families. Look at the home where I placed my Son, and hear what it is that the Spirit has to say to the church about blended families." The home where God placed his Son was a blended family: Jesus had four brothers and several sisters (Matthew 13:55-56). God was Jesus' Father; Joseph was the stepfather.

"The home where I placed my Son," says God, "is a home where I was honored." "Every year," says verse 41 of our text, "the parents of Jesus went to Jerusalem for the Feast of Passover." Going to the house of God and worshiping with others were expected family activities in Jesus' day. Please notice that the verse says "every year." There was no question such as, "Well, do you think we ought to go to church this time?" "I don't know; you know, the Capernaum Bulls are competing against the Palestine Trailblazers for the NBA (that's the Nazarene Basketball Association) championship. And I was thinking, maybe we ought to let the boy see the game this year. You know, all his friends will be watching it." There was no, "Honey, over at the Galilee Mall they're having the Super Sabbath Sale, and I was wondering, would you mind if I miss the service?"

Every time the saints met, the family went. In fact, they were so used to Jesus being with the other kids that they had traveled a whole day before they missed him. His home was a home where

God was honored. And church wasn't something that started when the boy became old enough to understand and make a decision for himself. You know, some of us have become confused. You don't give Junior a choice about going to school. Why do you give him a choice about going to church?

Verse 21 tells us that Jesus' parents took him to the temple to observe the religious custom of circumcision when he was a week old.[2] They positioned him in the precincts of the holy from the time he could be carried outside of his house. His home was a home where God was honored. They listened to what Simeon said about their son. They heard with awe what the woman preacher Anna said as she praised God for his presence. His home was a home where God was honored.[3]

If you are going to build a home for a blended family, it seems like the first thing God is saying is that there is some good news if you make your home a home where God is honored.

A Home Where God Is Central

The home where the Son of God was placed was a home where God was central. The relationship that both of these adults—Joseph and Mary—had with God was intact and in place before the baby was born. In fact, before they became physically intimate, they had a solid relationship with God. (If we could master this one principle, we could significantly reduce the risk of HIV infection.) God was central in their lives; God was central in their home. Look at Luke 1:34, where Mary said to the angel, "I am a virgin. How, then, can this be?" Matthew 1:18 tells us that "Mary was engaged to Joseph, but before they were married she found out that she was going to have a baby by the Holy Spirit." Verse 25 says, "But he had no sexual relations with her before she gave birth to her son."

Joseph, you will remember, was trying to figure out a way to get out of this sticky situation—and it *was* sticky! His woman was pregnant, and they weren't married. And he knew the baby wasn't his. What would people say? What *did* people say? You know they talked about them. Some folks still don't believe that Holy Ghost story. "Well, I don't mean any harm, but I've seen brother Judas hanging around there an awful lot." "Not the trustee?" "Umm-hmm."

"And Peter's mouth ain't no prayer book, honey. Have you heard him cuss?" "But you know Rev. Andrew is the quiet one, and you've got to watch those quiet ones, baby." "Umm-hmm!" "You got the right one, baby." "Umm-hmm!" Folk talked about them. And Joseph was trying to find a way out that would not disgrace his lady.

Then God told him, "Joseph, descendent of David, do not be afraid to take Mary to be your wife. For it is by the Holy Spirit that she has conceived" (Matthew 1:20). God was central in his life. God was central in their home. And that says that if you have a blended family, you have a head start if the Holy is headquartered in your home. Parenting children who are not your own is made easier when God is central in your home.

I cannot count the numbers of church members who have shared with me how "Big Mama" or "Muddear" always had enough food to feed what seemed like all the extra children on the block. She could take in all the strays and always had enough food and love to go around. When you look to the Lord as the provider of food, as the source and supply of love, love abounds. When God is central in the home, grace and mercy are much-cherished lessons. When God is central in the home, forgiveness becomes far more than some abstract concept; it becomes a lived reality day by day. When God is central in the home, trust becomes the tapestry that binds disparate lives together.

One of the preachers at the Hampton Ministers Conference[4] reminded us of a true story. He told of a tour guide from his church who was taking a group of African Americans to West Africa to learn about their roots and heritage. They saw Senegal, Dakar, and Gorée Island. They saw the slave forts and the Soumbedioune Market in Dakar (a large arts-and-crafts market). They saw Sierra Leone and Abidjan, and after leaving that sprawling city with its magnificent skyscrapers and unbelievably wide streets—the main streets in Abidjan are about as wide as our interstates—they went out into the bush to visit some people who lived very close to nature.

These bush people were allegedly master weavers. I say "allegedly" because when the African Americans came upon them to watch them weave, the tapestry they were weaving was unbelievably ugly. There was no symmetry. The colors were a hodgepodge, mixed up and mixed in. There was no design, and the pattern made no sense. As a matter of fact, it really looked slipshod. Some of the people cut their pieces at different lengths so that they were sloppy and uneven. The tapestry looked a mess.

One of the church members asked, "Why are they wasting their time on that mess? Why don't they just throw that one away and start all over again? Maybe they can get the next one right." The tour guide translated and whispered this outsider's question to the one in charge of the weaving. The one in charge looked up, smiled, gave a command in their native language, and, at the command, the workers flipped the weaving over—and there was the most beautiful, breathtaking work of art you could ever hope to see! The underside looked awful, but the top was awesome.

And that's how God works trust into the tapestry of the blended family. Many times what we see from the underside looks a mess, and we wonder why we're wasting our time, why we don't just give it up and perhaps start all over or admit we blew it and walk away from it with integrity. But that's just how we see it from the underside. From the other side, God shows us that *all* things work together for good to those who love the Lord, who keep God central, and are called according to his purpose (see Romans 8:28). When God is central in the home, trust becomes the tapestry that binds disparate lives together.

A Home Where God Is in Control

That home was a home where God was honored; it was a home where God was central; and it was also a home where God was in control. Joseph did what the Lord said to do because God was in control. Mary yielded her life to the Lord because God was in control. Jesus knew what he knew (from that home) to such an extent that he could amaze the Jewish teachers. He was raised in a home where God was in control.

In a home where God is in control—I don't care what the configuration of your blended family—I've got some good news for you. If you listen to the voice of God and not to what the people say, you'll be all right. In a home where God is in control, if you worship at the house of God like the Lord's parents did every time they had an opportunity, if you model and teach the will of God so your children and your stepchildren can talk with their teachers about important issues of life, then you won't have anything to worry about. Everything will be found and kept in divine order because God will take care of you.

"Be not dismayed whate'er betide"—"Joseph! Joseph! They're talking about your wife." It doesn't matter. God will take care of it. "Mary, the other children are looking kind of funny at that child with that other father." It doesn't matter. God will take care of it. Ever since the days of chattel slavery, black families have had all kinds of obstacles to overcome and stereotypes to live with, with marriage ruled out as an option and loved ones sold away at will. But it does not matter; God will take care of you.

Children, if you are in a blended family and they talk about you, remember they talked about Jesus. Hold your head up! Put a smile on your face. Step tall! Walk proud! Don't you hang your head down. Throw your shoulders back and say, "God will take care of me because I'm his child."

Devotional

Songs of Praise
Prayer
Scripture: Luke 2:41-52
Song: "God Is So Good"

Study Questions

1. What are some of the reservations that men and women have about marrying someone who already has children?

2. What are some fears that children have about their parents marrying or remarrying?

3. What role should in-laws and grandparents play in the decision to marry someone with children?

4. How can a person respond to other family members who frown on the formation of a blended family?

5. In what ways is Joseph a good example for a stepparent?

6. Blended families can be encouraged because the "author and finisher of our faith," Jesus himself, was the product of a blended family. This fact has many positive implications for ministry to blended families. In a society that has defined the nuclear family of Dad, Mom, and two biological children as the norm, what does Jesus' example have to offer those families that are constructed differently?

7. Given the hardships and legacy of slavery in the United States and its devastating effects on the slaves' family life, would you challenge the notion of what is "normal" for family construction within the African American community? For example, would you argue that the extended family—grandparents, aunts, uncles living together and participating in child rearing—is more the norm than the nuclear family? Would you argue that bonds of love are more normal than or just as normal as bonds of blood?

8. What are some practical ways in which we can make God central in our homes?

9. Examine your home. Is God in control?

10. What do you think was demonstrated by the story of the African tapestry weavers?

Good News for Bad Kids

1 Samuel 2:12-17; 8:1-5

Introduction

First Samuel 2:12 says, "The sons of Eli were scoundrels. They paid no attention to the LORD." First Samuel 8:1-3 says, "When Samuel grew old, he made his sons judges in Israel. The older son was named Joel and the younger one Abijah; they were judges in Beersheba. But they did not follow their father's example." Two times within a few short chapters, we are given a glimpse of some boys who are just plain old bad kids!

First Samuel 1, where the story of Hannah and Elkanah begins, says that Elkanah went with his family each year to offer sacrifices to the Lord at Shiloh. The chronicler[1] mentions in passing that Hophni and Phinehas, the two sons of Eli, were priests of the Lord. We do not know until later why the storyteller mentions their names, but we soon find out that even the offering being given by someone as sincere and as thankful as Hannah is being ripped off by some boys who are just plain old bad kids.

Their daddy, Eli, was the pastor of the church at Shiloh. Is there a daddy's heart that does not hope that one day his child will follow in his footsteps and take over the work that he started? This is especially so in the ministry. There are a lot of jokes told about ministers; everybody knows at least one. Yet, for those of us who prepare ourselves and deny ourselves, present ourselves and offer ourselves for service to the church, the ministry is a lonely profession, a misunderstood occupation, and an awfully isolated walk as one tries to follow the Lord and parent a family all at the same time.

Each year as you see beaming, bright, beautiful, young black youth heading into college—some to be doctors, some to be lawyers, some to write computer programs and become systems analysts, some in science and technology, some in nuclear physics and robotics—you scan the horizon wondering if anyone has heard a call from the Lord. Will anyone respond to a call to ministry? Does anyone respect the profession of ministry deeply enough or seriously enough to say, "Yes, that's what I want to do with my life"?

I've heard children in church talk about how they wanted to be one thing or another—*anything* but a preacher. I have read youngsters' essays on the black heroes they respected and admired, people they looked up to and wanted to be like, and unless it was a Nobel Peace-prize winner like Martin Luther King, Jr., or a presidential candidate like Jesse Jackson or a mysterious movement leader like Malcolm X, almost never did anyone want to be a pastor like Eli.

This is not your most sought-after job. So you know that a daddy looks with pride when one of his own children says yes to the Lord, yes to service, yes to sacrifice, yes to preaching, yes to pastoring, yes to the same number of years in school that a doctor or a lawyer spends with no chance of ever making one-tenth of what those professions pay. When a preacher's kid says yes to preaching, that is a proud moment.

We Spend Enough Painful Moments

We spend enough painful moments, moments when our families don't understand us, moments when our friends walk away from us, moments when our 'gotta do's' get in the way of our 'wanna do's'. We spend enough painful moments.

One Sunday we had our three services, and then I had to attend a graduation. My first appointment on Monday morning was at 7:30 A.M. I left the church building that night at 10:30 and left Rev. Barbara[2] here still working. When one of our members' brothers was killed, the family called at 1:20 A.M. Tuesday morning. Rev. Barbara was still at church.

That week I had to preach in Washington, D.C., for the Coalition of Black Preachers Responding to the Criminal Justice System and Its Treatment of African American Males. I had to speak three times that Friday: the United Charities Conference on the Family, a funeral for a young man killed in anger, and a graduation for poor black kids who are predicted to fail before they even get started. I had a retreat with my officers, and my body wouldn't go when I put it in drive and released the brakes.

I still had a speech to give for an organization, five services the next Sunday, and a sermon on prayer to finish up. And with my legs aching and my heart aching, I looked out the back window and saw my twenty-two-month-old excitedly playing with her grandfather. It was a painful moment. I was thankful to God that she had a granddaddy to spend time and enjoy life with her. I was grateful that she had a man to play with her, to throw the ball to her, to call out names to her: "tree," "bird," "water." I was grateful; yet, it was painful all at the same time because the thought came to me, "You don't even have time to play with your own child."

We spend enough painful moments.

Over that weekend, while other daddies were taking their kids to the ball game, to the Bulls game, taking their sons to the ballpark, my son and I were on our way to the United Negro College Fund Dinner, and my son still does not understand who Bill Gray[3] is and what it meant to shake Bill Gray's hand. His friends were out dancing. Why did he have to shake Bill Gray's hand? His attitude was, "Who is Bill Gray, anyway?"

We spend enough painful moments. Lord, grant us every now and then a peaceful, powerful, proud moment.

Eli's Bad Kids

And a proud moment is exactly what Eli—the preacher, the pastor, the priest—felt when two of his sons started serving in the house of the Lord. The only problem was that his kids were just plain old bad kids! They started off all right. They had a good home in which to grow. They had religious parents who trained them well. They had a mom and a daddy who taught them about the Lord, took them to church, taught them to pray, and sang the songs of Zion with them. Their parents told them about Abraham, Isaac, Jacob, Joseph, Moses, Joshua, Deborah, Miriam, Rachel, and Ruth. They had it all in their home: devotions and divinity, fun and faith, the work of God and the man of God. They started off all right, but look how they ended up.

We read in verses 12 and 17 that they were stealing from God. What we did not read was in verse 22, where they were stealing what singer Anita Baker calls "sweet love." Look at 1 Samuel 2:22: "Eli was now very old. He kept hearing about everything his sons were doing to the Israelites and that they were even sleeping with the women who worked at the entrance to the Tent of the LORD's presence." The preachers were sleeping with the doorkeepers. Lord have mercy! These were some bad kids—bad seeds, that's all. They started off all right, but look how they ended up.

Eli said to them, "Why are you doing these things? Everybody tells me about the evil you are doing. Stop it, my sons! This is an awful thing the people of the LORD are talking about! If a man sins against another man, God can defend him; but who can defend a man who sins against the LORD?" (v. 23).

Eli gave some sound advice. Eli offered excellent counsel. Eli talked to his children like many of you talk to your children. I've heard you talk to them. "Straighten up and fly right." "You'd better leave the cocaine alone." "You'd better put that reefer down." "You'd better come away from that crowd that's killing you." "Everything that's good to you ain't automatically or necessarily good for you." "If that man catches you fooling around with his lady . . ." "If you don't leave that woman's man alone . . ." "That narcotic's done made you null and void." "You'd better take time to know her." "Can two walk together unless they be agreed?" "You shouldn't marry anybody who's unevenly yoked with you. Do, and you're heading for trouble." "I know he looks good, but that fine hunk you see is just the house he lives in. Find out who lives on the inside; there are a whole lot of monsters living in mansions." "What goes around comes around."

Eli talked to his children like you and I talk to our children. Verse 25 says, however, "But they would not listen to their father." They were just bad kids, that's all.

Rev. Susan Williams Smith, now Dr. Smith, in one of her last sermons while she was on staff here said that a lot of us are running around wringing our hands, trying to figure out what we did to make our children turn out the way they did when the answer many times is, "Nothing!" You've just got bad kids, that's all. Face it. Some of our kids didn't grow up the way they were raised or trained. They decided to do something else all on their own. And Eli is not alone in this. In just a few short verses we see Samuel's sons doing just like Eli's sons. Bad kids!

Bad Kids Ignore Good Parental Models

What are the characteristics of bad kids? Well, bad kids ignore their parental models. Chapter 2 says that Eli's sons "would not listen to their father" (v. 25), and chapter 8 says Samuel's sons "did not follow their father's example" (v. 3). They ignored their parental models. How about that chapter in your life?

Some of us ignored our parental models. Our parents were in church every time the doors opened. Now, they must have been getting something there for the inside that made all the difference in the world for this life on the outside. But we could not pick up on that. All we knew was that once we got grown, we weren't going to ever be in church all day long. We ignored our parental models. In what chapter of your life did you ignore your good parental models?

Bad children do their own things and go their own way. Our parents, many of them, tried to teach us to walk in the straight and narrow way. Our parents tried to get us to follow him who says, "I am the way." But not us. Oh no! Not the kid! Our parents tried to get us to do it God's way, but we just had to do it our way. Bad kids.

Bad kids ignore parental models. Bad kids do their own thing and go their own way. Bad kids violate the religious traditions of the elders. That's what Hophni and Phinehas did. And do you realize, parenthetically, that Phinehas means "Pa-nihesi," which is Egyptian for "the Nubian," "the black"? This was a bad black boy. Hophni and Phinehas violated the religious tradition of the elders. Samuel's sons did their thing, too. They did not follow their father's example. They violated the religious tradition of the elders.

Before we come down too hard on these boys, we need to look at our own lives. In our tradition, we prayed early in the morning, and we were not ashamed to call on the name of the Lord. But conversely, as I recently reminded some high school students, in our day and age, some black people call God "Allah" and say "*As salaam alaikum*."[4] In our day and age, some black people call God "Yahweh" and say "*Shalom alechem*."[5] In our day and age, some black people call God "Ra" and "Amon-Ra," and they greet each new day saying "*Hotep*."[6] But while some call him Allah and some call him Yahweh and some call him Ra and Amon-Ra, I call him "the joy of my salvation." I call him "Bread" when I'm hungry and "Water" when I'm thirsty. I call him "Bridge over Troubled Waters" and "Bright and Morning Star." Where some say "*As salaam alaikum*" and "*Shalom alechem*," "*Hotep*" and "*Kemet*,"[7] I say all the time, "Jesus, excellent is thy name." "Thank you, Jesus!" "Hallelujah!" "God is good." I'm sticking with our tradition.

I also reminded the students, "You don't need drugs. You don't need gangs. You don't need guns. All you need is God because God has everything you need." Some of us violate tradition. We put more stock in Gucci than we do in God. We put more faith in Coach than we do in Christ. We care more about our Benzes and Beemers than we do about the beams of heaven. We put more importance on where we live now than where we're going to spend eternity. We violate the religious tradition of the elders.

Our folks used to love church and stay in church all day long. Now we can't wait to get *out* of church. You invite folks to church now—just invite them—and the first thing they want to know is, "Well, what time are services over?" Tell them, "When they're over; that's when they're over." You don't ask, "What time is the party over?" Well, we're having a Jesus party, and it ain't over 'til it's over!

Bad kids ignore parental models, do their own thing, and go their own way. Bad kids ignore the love of God and disrespect the things of God and have lost all awe for the majesty and power of God.

Bad Kids Disrespect the Things of God

We read how Hophni and Phinehas treated the offerings. Remember, an offering is given in response to the love of God. When you ignore an offering, you are thumbing your nose at the love of God. "Now, Reverend, you don't understand." No, *you* don't understand. I see your seventy-five-dollar crimps, your eighty-dollar wrap, and your hundred-dollar shoes. You have your priorities mixed up, putting five dollars in the offering plate. Malachi 3:8 (RSV) says, "Will man rob God? Yet you are robbing me. . . . in your tithes and offerings." A "God robber" ignores the love of God and thumbs her nose at what God has given her. Hophni and Phinehas disrespected the things of God.

Verse 17 of chapter 2 says they treated the offerings to the Lord with much disrespect. We have lost a sense of the holy. We disrespect the things that belong to God. Don't you know that a tithe doesn't even belong to you? It belongs to God. A tithe is a debt I owe; an offering is a seed I sow. We disrespect those things that belong to God. We disrespect the precincts of the holy. We disrespect the sanctuary of God. We disrespect the Word of God, and we disrespect the men and women of God. Bad kids ignore the love of God, disrespect the things of God, and have lost all awe of the majesty and power of God.

It was like these boys had never heard of a God who could put a ram in the bushes,[8] a God who could put a baby in a barren womb,[9] a God who could put a slave in the number-two slot in the government,[10] a God who could put a dry highway in the middle of an angry sea,[11] a God who could bring down impregnable walls with nothing but a trumpet and a shout.[12] This God is a God to be held in awe and reverence. But bad kids think they can take God on and win. They have lost a sense of awe.

As we have looked at Eli's and Samuel's bad kids, I have been pointing out some parallels between them and us because I happen to know that some of us are bad kids. We may not be stealing the offerings like a tricky trustee or an underhanded usher. We may not be sleeping with the doorkeepers and lying with whomever we will, but we have ignored our parental models. We have done our own thing and gone our own way. We have violated the religious tradition of our elders, and we have ignored the love of God, lost respect for the things of God, and lost all awe for the majesty of God.

But I call your attention to the title of this sermon, which is "Good News for Bad Kids." God has some good news for those of us who are bad kids and for you parents who know you have some bad kids—and it's found right here in the text if you look at it from a different angle.

Good News for Bad Kids

Remember how the boys started out? They started out in good homes, like some of us. But they didn't end up the way they started out. The good news is: it's not how you start out that counts; it's how you end up that makes all the difference in the world.

I started out as a bad kid: arrested at age fifteen for grand larceny auto theft. I remember the pained look on my daddy's face the night he came to pick me up from the lockup. I told you preachers have more than their share of painful moments. I brought pain. I brought shame to my parents because I was a bad kid. We can't get some of our bad kids to come into the sanctuary on Sunday. They want to hang out somewhere else in the building and hang out in the street with their friends. But Mother or Father, don't you give up on Junior. You keep on praying. Hard as his head may be, you keep on praying. And don't you stop praying because look what God has done for me, in me, with me, and through me. It's not how you start out that counts but how you end up.

Some of you swore you weren't going to be found in anybody's church. Well, look where you ended up! Some of you swore you weren't ever going to get married. Look where you ended up! Some of you, once upon a time, were so far from being saved that you didn't even want to hear the language of the church anymore. Today, your soul looks back and sings not only, "How I got over," but, "If it had not been for the Lord on my side, where would I be?"

God fixed it with grace. God fixed it on Calvary. God fixed you with Jesus, and God has filled you with the Holy Ghost. One writer put it this way: "When I think of the goodness of Jesus and all that he's done for me, well my soul says, 'Lord, I thank you.'" For all that he's done, I thank him. He put food on my table, hope in my heart, clothes on my back, running in my feet, and a roof over my head. I thank him.

Answer this question: Do you like Michael Jordan? Do you like Scotty Pippen? Do you like B. J. and Stacey, Craig Hodges and Livingston?[13] Well, Michael didn't die for you. Scotty didn't give his life for you. B. J. is no bridge over troubled water, and Stacey can't stand in a storm with you. You ought to praise God. Say, "Lord, I thank you."

Devotional

Songs of Praise
Prayer
Scripture: 1 Samuel 2:12-17; 8:1-5
Song: "Thank You, Lord"

Study Questions

1. Who is to blame for bad kids? Parents? Society? Peer groups? The kids themselves?

2. What are some strategies offered here for dealing with bad kids?

3. How can a good parent or guardian who has done all within his or her power to rear a good child be released from guilt if that child turns bad?

4. Is it ever appropriate to give up on a so-called bad child? Did David give up on Absalom (2 Samuel 16:15–18:33)? Did Eli and Samuel give up on their sons (1 Samuel 2:12-17; 3:11-13; 8:1-5)?

5. Do children ever become too old or too grown to receive the counsel of their parents or elders?

6. How can a parent or guardian help a child who will not listen to good advice?

7. Why is it important to continue to be a good role model even if it seems that the child is not paying attention?

8. Do you believe in Proverbs 22:6 (KJV): "Train up a child in the way he should go: and when he is old, he will not depart from it"? Can you give some examples of people you know who strayed from good training, but, like the prodigal son, later "came to themselves" and began to live right?

9. Why do you think it might be necessary for some young people to reject the religious traditions of their elders?

10. What can parents and guardians do to alleviate their own frustrations and anxieties while they are waiting for their bad kids to "come to themselves"?

Good News for Good Fathers

Genesis 48:8-22

Introduction

[One day] Joseph was told that his father, [Jacob], was ill. So he took his two sons, Manasseh and Ephraim, and went to see Jacob. When Jacob was told that his son Joseph had come to see him, he gathered his strength and sat up in bed. Jacob said to Joseph, "Almighty God appeared to me at Luz in the land of Canaan and blessed me. He said to me, 'I will give you many children, so that your descendants will become many nations; I will give this land to your descendants as their possession forever.' " Jacob continued, "Joseph, your two sons, who were born to you in Egypt before I came here, belong to me; Ephraim and Manasseh are just as much my sons as Reuben and Simeon" (Genesis 48:1-5).

Like bad parents, much has been written about bad fathers. The focus is on bad fathers to such an extent that we tend to forget that there are some *good* fathers. In fact, those of us who have good fathers or who had good fathers tend to be made to feel guilty by all the bad-mouthing others do about their bad fathers. "You can't tell me nothing 'bout no black man, girlfriend. I can write the book on them." We can emphasize bad fathers to the point that we ignore the fact that there are good ones, too.

The Word of God has something to say about what it takes to be a good father. When I was a little boy, I didn't understand what

I had right in front of me. I did not understand what God had put right in the home beside me. Sometimes, you know, we cannot see the forest for the trees.

Looking for Role Models

Bill Cosby said a few years back that in all this push and drive for positive male role models for our young boys and positive images for our young girls, we keep looking in the wrong place. We look at basketball players like Michael Jordan and Scotty Pippen. We look at prizefighters like Mike Tyson and Evander Holyfield. We look at athletes and sports figures. We look at sex symbols like Billy Dee Williams, Richard Roundtree, or Wesley Snipes. We are looking in the wrong places. We made Magic Johnson our hero. We made Michael Jordan our hero. We made Bill Cosby our hero. And when Magic slips or Michael gambles or Bill has a bad day, we are devastated because our heroes and role models have fallen from their pedestals.

Well, says Cosby, the first problem is that we put our human beings and heroes up on a pedestal, and no one alive belongs on a pedestal. Only an inanimate object like a statue or something we made in our image belongs on a pedestal. Anything or anyone God made belongs in the dirt with us. God made us from dirt, and even though we are dirt dignified by divinity—made in God's image—we are not to be worshiped as gods; we are to worship God.

The second problem is that we have ignored the greatest role model God has given us: the man right there in our home who gets up every day and goes to work whether he feels like it or not, the man who helps us tie our shoes or who, like Carl Tutt (one of Trinity's members), takes time to read to his children. When I called for Carl one evening, his wife said, "He and I are sitting here having a private conversation. Do you want to interrupt my time with my husband?" The next time I called, I said, "Are you having a private conversation?" She said, "No, he's reading to the children." So I told her not to disturb him. "Tell him I'll call him tomorrow at the office."

The man who comes home in the evenings, who helps with his children's homework, the man who draws pictures and goes to school programs, the man who never has his name in neon lights but who signs his name on the mortgage and the tuition vouchers, the man who puts up with our moods and our missteps and our mistakes and our misconceptions, the man who rides us horsey and teaches us hambone, the man who sings to us and lectures to us and keeps on loving us even when we are unlovable—*that man* is the greatest role model God has given us. Yet we keep on ignoring that God-given role model, chasing after some illusory, man-made, media-made image with whom we can never come into contact or share our lives. These daddies in our homes are the greatest role models, many of them, and God gave me one.

God put a daddy in my house for whom I will go to my grave being thankful. But when I was little, I did not understand this. I did not understand what I had right there in front of me. My daddy would not let me have some cap pistols that my uncle brought for me. All the other boys had guns, so I didn't understand. I thought it took a gun to make a man, and my daddy was trying to teach me that it didn't take a gun to make a man; it took a God to make a man. My peers were teaching me that being a man was a function of my sexuality, and my papa was trying to get me to see that being a man was a function of my spirituality.

My grandson brought this lesson home for me recently. He climbed into bed with me early in the morning, and the first thing he did was rub my arm and look at it, and then he asked me, "Granddaddy, are you black?" And it hit me as he asked that God looks not as we look on the outward appearances, but God looks at the heart. My grandson was trying to understand, based upon complexion, but my God knows and understands based upon condition and conviction. My grandson was basing his question on what he could see, but my God had the answer based on what *he* could see. It takes a God to make a man. It takes a God to make a black man.

Then my grandson said, "Grandpa, let me see your muscle. Mine is like steel. Yours is like a wet noodle." American images of masculinity! His world is made up of Ninja Turtles, Raphael, and karate chops. That's what it takes to be considered a man in the nineties. In 1952, it took a six-shooter and a fast draw. Today, it takes an Uzi, an AK47, your hat worn to the right side, and your hip-hop slang said right—"Yo!" These are meaningless symbols pointing to the outside, and nothing of substance that deals with the inside.

Being a man is a function of your spirituality. That's what my dad was trying to teach, and that's what the Word of God is trying to teach.

A Good Father Puts God First

A good father is a man who puts God first. Not his kids. Not his wife. Not his loves. Not his likes or his looks but his Lord. God comes first in his life. Putting God first is what Joseph modeled in his life. He kept God central. From the time he got in trouble with his brothers by telling them what God showed him till the time he got in trouble with his boss's wife by telling her that pleasing God meant more than feeling good, Joseph was a man who kept God central. Look at what he named his sons: Manasseh ("God has made me forget my sufferings") and Ephraim ("God has given me children in the land of my trouble"). In both instances, God is in the naming of his sons. God is in the creation of his deliverance. God is in the center of his situation. He kept God central in order to keep his sanity.

A Good Father Seeks God's Guidance

Putting God first means keeping God central and seeking God's guidance. Joseph sought God's guidance every step of the way. When disliked by his brothers, he sought God's guidance. When put in a pit, he sought God's guidance. When tempted by a woman, he sought God's guidance. When thrown into prison, he sought God's guidance. Whether up or down, he sought God's guidance. When shown the divine plan, he sought God's guidance. When questioned by the king, he sought God's guidance. When elevated to the administration, he sought God's guidance. When dealing with his brothers, he sought God's guidance.[1]

How would you make out if you had to deal with folk who hated you? Folk who lied on you? Folk who put you in a pit? Folk who threw stumbling blocks in your way? Folk who didn't care if you lived or died? Sounds like an ordinary life of an ordinary black person! Joseph sought the Lord's guidance as he was faced with those situations. How many times do I remember hearing my daddy pray, "Father, I stretch my hand to thee. No other help I know." He was seeking the Lord's guidance.

My daddy came from the tobacco fields of Caroline County, Virginia, to a municipal board seat, the only black on the Juvenile Detention and Rehabilitation Board for the city of Philadelphia. But he never got too grand to seek God's guidance. He went to college with only a quarter in his pocket, and he earned the Bachelor of Theology, the Bachelor of Arts, and the Master of Divinity from Virginia Union. Then he earned the Master of Sacred Theology from the Lutheran School of Theology. But he never got so educated that he stopped seeking God's guidance.

Every midweek prayer service, my daddy was there seeking God's guidance. Every morning that the good Lord sent and still sends, he's at our breakfast table, his devotional guide in one hand, his Bible in the other hand, his hand in God's hand. My daddy started off—and still starts off—every day seeking God's guidance. Every decision he had to make—decisions concerning the church, decisions concerning his officers, decisions concerning his profession, decisions concerning his family—was made after seeking the Lord's guidance.

The Lord knows how I wish I had learned from him while I had the model right there in front of me! That would have saved a lot of heartache and heartbreak and prevented me from making some bad decisions that I made by getting out in front of God. If only I had sought the Lord's guidance.

A Good Father Asks for God's Blessings

A good father keeps God central, seeks God's guidance, and asks for God's blessings. Joseph, in the passage that we read together, is bringing his two sons to their grandfather to receive God's blessings. He's asking that the Lord bless the days of his sons' lives. I cannot remember a day that our family was sent out into a mean, cruel, and racist world without asking the Lord's blessings. My daddy asked God's blessings on our every move, our every day, our every deed, our every task, our every step.

Did you stop to ask God's blessings upon your day this morning? We take so many things for granted. We get up in the morning and rush out the door, barely kissing each other good-bye, never stopping to think that we may never come back in that door again. We need to ask God's blessings on our day. We need to ask God's blessings on our traveling to and fro. I've flown over two thousand miles in a weekend, and I know it's no one but God who keeps that big bird up in the sky. I ask God for his blessings, and I thank him for his blessings. Traveling can be just as dangerous by car or bus. There is no guarantee that when we walk down that aisle one Sunday that we won't be rolled down that same aisle the next Sunday. We need to ask God for his blessings and stop taking God for granted. David said that "the steps of a good man are ordered by the LORD."[2] A good man, a good father, puts God first. He keeps God central, he seeks God's guidance, and he asks for God's blessings.

A Good Father Puts the Past Behind Him

A good father puts the past behind him. You can't go back and relive the past. The past is past. You can't go back and get all those folk who got you when you were coming along. You can't go back and undo what has already been done. The past is past.

Again, Joseph gives us the biblical model. Joseph learned from the mistakes of the past. He is a different son here. He is a different brother here in this sermon text than the son and brother he was in chapter 37. You can learn from the mistakes of the past. If you made a mistake, don't try to deny it. Try to learn from it. There is always a lesson to be learned from a lousy set of circumstances. Look at what happened. Look at what you did wrong. Look at what was done wrong to you, and then learn from it. Don't live *in* it. Learn *from* it. Have you ever sat down to review the failures of your past? Not to dwell on them and start feeling down on yourself but to see what lessons the Lord would have you learn from them?

Who hurt you when you did not deserve to be hurt? Who lied about you when you had done nothing to deserve that kind of treatment? Who? Fix your mind on those persons now. Are you focusing on them? Now, let them go! Release them so you can be whole. Learn from what they did. Don't lie on a pallet of pity. Take up your bed and walk! Learn from the pain, and be a better you for the experience. If you want to know what to do with your past, learn from the mistakes of your past; then let the past be the past.

If it's over, it's over. Let it be over. Don't go back and drag it up, dig it up, and carry it around. It's a corpse, badly decomposed and stinking. Let it stay buried.

There was an elderly black woman who kept a sweet disposition no matter what happened. She didn't have one of those saved-and-sanctified saccharin smiles, phoney as the day is long. She didn't grin in your face and gossip all over town about you. No, this sister was genuinely sweet, no matter what she was going through. Heartache? Her disposition was sweet. Disappointment? Her disposition was sweet. Child on drugs? Her disposition was sweet. More month left than she had money left? Her disposition stayed sweet. And somebody asked her, "How are you able to keep on smiling when I know what's going on in your life?" She said, "Because of what the Bible says." "What does the Bible say?" "It says, 'And it came to *pass*.' This ain't gonna be always. It didn't come to *stay*. It came to *pass*." I'm so glad that trouble don't last always! And once it has passed, let it be past. Let the past be past.

Joseph said, "What you did to me in the past, you meant for evil, but God turned it into good."[3] Look at it in a different light. Paul said, "All things work together for good to them that love God."[4] Look at your past in that light. He said, "This one thing I do, forgetting those things which are behind, and reaching forth unto those things which are before, I press toward the mark . . ."[5] Look at your past in that light. Is the path of your past all crooked and out of line? Remember, God can take a crooked stick and hit a straight lick. A good father puts God first. A good father puts his past behind him.

Good Fathers Put Their Trust in the Lord

Joseph put his trust in God. When he couldn't see how things were going to turn out, he didn't give up. He gave it to God. He put his trust in God. In a subterranean pit,[6] he put his trust in God. In Potiphar's house,[7] he put his trust in God. In the prison house,[8] he put his trust in God. The wine steward left and forgot all about him, let him down, and left him right where he found him.[9] But Joseph's faith, thank God, was not in a wine steward who tasted the wine. His hope was in the One who *made* the grapes for the wine. He put his trust in God. And his life shows us that trusting in God is not always easy.

Sometimes you have to trust God when it doesn't make any sense to do so. Sometimes you have to trust God when there are no visible signs in your life or on the horizon that give you any hope to hold on for any reason. It isn't always easy.

Joseph had no "because of's" in his life. Hated by his brothers, thrown in a pit, sold into slavery, lied on by a lady, put into a prison, forgotten by a friend, he trusted not *because of*, but *in spite of*. Like Job, he said, "Though he slay me, yet will I trust in him."[10] I like that. I like that because God has been too good to me for me to give up on him. When everything isn't going my way, I trust God anyhow. I sing hallelujah anyhow. I say, "Thank you, Jesus," anyhow.

Putting trust in God means, first of all, that it isn't always easy. Second, it means trusting not because of but in spite of. But most of all, it means taking your hands off of it and putting it in God's hands. Your home, your hopes, your hurts—put them in God's hands; your dreams, your life, your future—in God's hands; your children, your finances, your family—in God's hands; your failures, your heartaches, and your problems—in God's hands. And then take your hands off, confident that God can handle what you are not able to handle. When you *can't*, God *can*. Put it all in God's hands.

Devotional

Songs of Praise
Prayer
Scripture: Genesis 48:8-22
Song: "I Will Trust in the Lord"

Study Questions

1. What can be done in our homes, schools, churches, and civic organizations to promote the idea that earnest, dependable, hard-working men who take care of their families and responsibilities are the best role models for boys and girls?

2. Bill Cosby probably did not think that he was saying something that would be considered newsworthy when he suggested that the kind of men described in the previous question were more worthy of being called role models than the stars who are promoted in the media. Why did Cosby's comment attract so much attention? How and why have media images replaced "real people" as role models for children and youth?

3. Consider the images of masculinity for boys mentioned in this sermon. Are these harmless images that are part of a boy's passage into manhood, or are they harmful images that distort the real meaning of manhood?

4. What can the church do to promote positive development in boys and girls so that they will become mature men and women?

5. Should Christians copy the world's style (Christian rap, Christian gangs) in order to compete with what society is offering our youth today, especially our young men?

6. What were some of the costs that Joseph had to pay for putting God first? What were some of the blessings he reaped for putting God first?

7. What are some costs that good fathers will pay today for putting God first in situations that may be similar to Joseph's? What are some blessings that good fathers will reap?

8. Name some situations that would call for a good father to seek

God's guidance. What steps should he follow in seeking guidance from God?

9. Read James 5:16 and Ephesians 5:23-27. What is the father's role in obtaining God's blessings for his family?

10. Many people have said that the problems our youth face today are due to the absence of fathers in the home. HUD secretary Henry Cisneros once said that good mothers notwithstanding, it takes a strong father to effectively rear children, especially boys. Can mothers offer to children the same things that fathers can offer? If there are differences in what each parent has to offer, what are some of those differences?

Good News for Bad Fathers

2 Samuel 13:1-18a

Introduction

We read in our text the sad and sordid story of two brothers and a sister who break their daddy's heart by behavior that is almost too despicable to be repeated among decent folk. Incest leads to murder, rape, estrangement, and alienation. Shame and disgust drive a family to destruction and despair. And what you miss if you start the story here is the awful truth that a lot of us live with day in and day out.

So let's back up to chapter 11, to a story that is well known. It is the story of a man and a woman who share sweet love. Who hasn't been in love? There is something mystifying about love. Just seeing the person you love sometimes can make a difference in your day or your week. Just a smile, just a look, and you're messed up for days! Sometimes you can just hear his or her name and your heart will skip a beat. Several years back—back in the days when they used to *sing* songs rather than rap them—I think it was Chuck Jackson who used to sing a song, one line of which said, "Speak her name and I grow misty-eyed." Just the name is all it takes.

Well, this man and this woman in 2 Samuel 11 who shared sweet love only had a couple of major problems. First, he was married to somebody else. Second, she was married to somebody else. Her husband was away in the military, and he (the man in the drama) was a pistol anyway, so nobody paid much attention to his philandering.

They had a ball until the inevitable happened—she got pregnant. And then their stuff started to unravel. What do you do when you end up pregnant and you haven't slept with your husband in months? Can't you see them huddling together trying to get their stories straight, trying to get their lie together. What do you do? What *can* you say? How do you get out of this predicament?

King David (the man in our drama) came up with what he thought was the perfect plan. He would get Bathsheba's husband home on leave, let him sleep with his wife, and then pray that the baby would look like the mama. Besides, she could always say that the baby was premature. Nobody would know any different, and everything would be all right. So he arranged for an emergency leave for the husband. Uriah, Bathsheba's husband, came home and had a nice little chat with his commander-in-chief. The only problem was that when he went home, he didn't go to bed with his wife. You feel the tension mounting in this story as she reports back to her lover, "It didn't work. He didn't touch me."

The king then tries to get him drunk. You know what they say, "Candy is dandy, but liquor is quicker." Get him drunk. He'll forget all that gung-ho talk then and take care of business, or at least we can *tell* him he took care of business. If we get him drunk enough, he won't know the difference. Can I get an "amen" from folk who have been drunk? You don't know what you did! Somebody tells you. Yeah, you did it! So King David gave him about ten Long Island iced teas. "Have another drink of liquor. Have another drink." The only problem was the man didn't even go home. He stayed at the palace and slept it off. The level of tension moves about six notches higher now. "What are we going to do?"

When mischief didn't work, it was time for murder. "We tried to con him, we tried to coax him, we tried to be coy with him, and none of that worked. So, since conning and coaxing and coyness failed, it's killing time. Let's kill him; get him out of the way. Then you and I can be together. We can use that same premature story to cover our stuff." And so they did.

But God has this tendency of reminding us every now and then that you can get *by*, but you can't get away. Joe Louis, the great black boxer, used to put it this way: "You can run, but you can't hide." God sent a word to the king that he was not pleased with the sin. God is never pleased with our sin. And, in that word that God sent (2 Samuel 12:10), God says, "Now"—and this is the verse you need to read before reading that awful story about Tamar—"Now, in every generation some of your descendants will die a violent death because you have disobeyed me and have taken Uriah's wife."

Fathers Set the Stage for Their Children's Life Drama

As we read what happened to Tamar,[1] what happened to Amnon,[2] and what happened to Absalom[3] and that sweet revenge, you must keep in mind this one verse—2 Samuel 12:10—or you'll miss the point so many daddies and mommies need to hear. The father's behavior, the father's morals, the father's example many times set the stage upon which the children act out the drama of their lives. Let me say that again: The father's behavior, the father's morals, the father's example many times set the stage upon which the children act out the drama of their lives.

David's actions started a chain reaction that was devastating and deadly in its implications. David was not the role model of a good father. David was one of the Bible's *many* bad fathers. His behavior set the stage for the tragedy that was acted out by his own children. Please observe, daddies: what our children see us do many times *does* affect, *does* shape, and *does* mold what they do.

During the Chicago blizzard of 1979, a man's car spun out of control on him on State Highway 137, up near the Great Lakes Naval Station. Stuck on the side of the road, with snow drifts too high for his eight-year-old son to walk in, the father told the boy to stay in the car until he came back with help. He cracked his windows to remove the possibility of carbon monoxide poisoning and left the motor running so his son would have plenty of heat. He walked the three miles to the base, but he had no idea as he walked that the fierce storm would prohibit him from getting back to his car for three days. The roads had become not just impassable but impossible. Nobody could tell where the fields stopped and the roads started. Fifty-mile-per-hour winds caused drifts ten to twenty feet high.

When the daddy realized that his son was stranded, he had to be physically restrained because he insisted on going back somehow to get his boy. But in the midst of his struggle to get free, he heard his son's voice in the next room in the warming center. In disbelief, he ran next door. There was his son, laughing and playing with the sailors and the other children. "Son, how did you get here?" he asked. "I thought you were still in the car." "It was easy, Daddy," said the son. "I was afraid to stay where you left me, so I waited until you were out of sight; then I followed, walking in your footsteps."

Fathers, somebody is watching where you're walking, and he or she is following in your footsteps. What our children see us do many times does affect, does mold, and does shape what they do. If they hear us talk holy and see us live whorish, it affects their beliefs about the church. If they see us praise God in church and raise hell at home, they begin to question what it is we believe.

David's pitiful performance as a man canceled out his masterful performance as a musician. David was one of the many bad fathers, and their names are legion. They are the men who make babies but do not help raise babies. They are the men who will knock a woman up and then put that same woman down. They are the men who have no time for homework and no time for the holy. They've got time for golf but no time for God. They've got time for the ladies but no time for the Lord. The two words that are not in their vocabularies are *commitment* and *responsibility*. You can't make them pay child support, and you can't count on them for emotional support. I am telling you, their names are legion.

When I announced that I was preaching a sermon on bad fathers, two members contacted me about their daddies, who never owned them while they were growing up. Their mamas were good enough to make love with but not to raise a family with. And, as a result, these members grew up knowing who their daddies were and wondering why their daddies never acknowledged them. Their names are legion.

Another member asked me if it was wrong for her not to respond lovingly to her daddy, who never gave her mama one red cent while she was growing up, but now that she's "thirty-something," wants to introduce her to his other children, have her come to the family reunion, and show off his baby girl. And she's having a hard time with that rascal. Their names are legion. Another member asked me what to do about her daddy who never loved her. She was "illegitimate," and it's taken him five years now since establishing contact with her—she's twenty-six—to spell her name correctly. Bad daddies are a dime a dozen, and their names are legion.

A Bad Father Is Selfish and Self-Centered

A bad father is a man who is selfish and self-centered. That's where David was when he saw Uriah's wife and sired a son by her. He didn't care anything about her marriage, her life, or her husband. He cared only about what *he* wanted, what *he* needed, and what *he* had to have. Selfish. Self-centered. Self is on the throne. Self is at the center of his life. A bad father puts himself first. A bad father doesn't even think about his children's needs; only what he needs is of paramount importance. And I don't mean just financial needs and material needs either. Children need that now, make no mistake. But they also need to be hugged. Children need to be helped. Children need to be held. Children need to know somebody is on their side, somebody is in their corner, somebody is pulling for them and praying for them. Children need to know that they are not alone in this world.

African American children especially need to know that this world will hound them, haunt them, and hate them because of the color of their skin and the texture of their hair. Derrick Bell's analysis of this situation is penetrating.[4] Dr. Bell maintains that racism is alive and well in this country. When he came to Chicago to speak, some white folks and a few colored folks got upset because he demonstrated so articulately that not only has racism always been in this country, it is still here, and—guess what—it's going to continue to be here. Folks were upset. They thought his premise was incredulous, impossible, absurd, and preposterous. After all, we were taught to sing, "We shall overcome." Bell said we need to stop singing and start working, but work from the premise that racism isn't going anywhere. He said that some white folks need racism to maintain their psychotic sanity.

They thought Derrick Bell was crazy. But that was before the Rodney King verdict.[5] This is a world in which my baby daughter will be hated because of her skin color. In this kind of world, she needs to know that God didn't make a mistake when he made her, that God didn't make junk when he made her, and that God made a star when he made her. African American children have special needs in this Eurocentric wasteland of lily-white lies and outright distortions. Our children have needs, and those needs must be met. But a bad father ignores everybody else's needs but his own. He is selfish and self-centered.

A Bad Father's Wants Overrule His Oughts

A bad father puts his wants ahead of his oughts, and most of the time he does not know the difference between want and need. When David saw Bathsheba's beauty, he placed no brakes on his behavior. They told him who she was. They told him she was married. And "ought" should have kicked in right there: "You *ought* to leave that alone. You *ought* to behave yourself. You *ought* to be ashamed of yourself. You *ought* not to fool with a married woman. You *ought* to be content with what you already have." But want overruled ought, and David went on to see about getting what he wanted. He wanted her, so he made his move.

Did he need her? He was already married to Saul's daughter, Michal. He already had his plate full. He already had more than he could handle, but want takes precedence over need. A bad father is selfish and self-centered. And a bad father puts his wants ahead of his oughts—and most of the time he does not know the difference between want and need.

Bad Fathers Don't Want to Act Saved

One of the most dangerous characteristics I have seen in bad fathers is that they want to *be* saved, but they don't want to *act* saved. You see, David is the same David who wrote, "The LORD is my light and my salvation."[6] David wanted to *be* saved, but he didn't want to *act* saved. Instead of singing, "Wait on the LORD: be of good courage,"[7] he was singing, "If loving you is wrong, I don't wanna do right." David wanted to be saved, but he didn't want to act saved. And some of us want to be saved, but we don't want to act saved. We're like St. Augustine, the African who prayed, "Lord, take away all my desire to sin." All but one. "Don't take that one yet." We want to *be* saved but not *act* saved.

When a guest evangelist comes and asks for people who want to be saved, some of us go forward every night. Saved five times a week. We want to *be* saved, but we don't want to *act* saved. When it comes to changing our habits and changing our hearts, changing our hangouts and changing our hang-ups, changing what we say and changing what we do—when it comes to holiness and living our lives in line with what the Word of God requires, we don't want to be saved—not if it means changing.

Good News for Bad Fathers

A bad father is selfish and self-centered. A bad father puts his wants ahead of his oughts and does not know the difference between want and need. A bad father wants to be saved, but he does not want to act saved.

So where is the "Good News for Bad Fathers"? The *good* news is that you don't have to go on like you've been going on. You can stop the way you've been heading and turn around and head in another direction. You can't do it under your own power, but if you have the will, God has the way. Jesus can turn your life around right now. That's good news! You don't have to keep going on like you've been going on. If you've been a bad father, the Lord can overturn the verdict on your punishment. The Lord can give you another chance.

Bad fathers, I have some good news. You don't have to end up like you started out. Jesus can change the ending of your story, and he can change it right now. "If the Son shall set you free, you shall be free indeed" (John 8:36). Some of us have messed up terribly. We've been sowing wild oats all over the place. But look at David praying in Psalm 51:1 (KJV): "Have mercy upon me, O God, according to thy lovingkindness." The Word shows that repentance of sins repeals the sentence: "Create in me a clean heart, O God; and renew a right spirit within me. Cast me not away from thy presence; and take not thy holy spirit from me. Restore unto me the joy of thy salvation" (vv. 11-12, KJV).

Good news! Repentance of sins repeals the sentence. But remember, brothers, it does not stop the crop. God will forgive us for sowing wild oats, but he isn't going stop the crop. No. What you sow, you reap. But God can make you over on the inside. The Lord can take what you bring him and make something brand new out of your failures. The Lord can change you from being a bad father into being a *former* bad father. The Lord can change you from being a drug addict into being a *former* drug addict. The Lord can change you from being an alcoholic into being a *former* alcoholic. The Lord can change you from being an ordinary sinner into being an extraordinary sinner saved by grace. The Lord can make your crooked places straight. The Lord can make your rough places plain. You need to come to him today. I have some good news for you: If you come to Jesus, *if you come to Jesus*, he can and he will change you right now.

Devotional

Songs of Praise
Prayer
Scripture: 2 Samuel 13:1-18a
Song: "Come to Jesus"

Study Questions

1. The sins of ungodly fathers are visited upon their children unto the third and fourth generation, according to the Ten Commandments (Exodus 20:5). What sins of the slave-master fathers of African Americans have been visited upon succeeding generations? What are some of the problems that African Americans have had to deal with that can be traced to the mass rape of African slave women by slave owners and overseers and their subsequent denial of paternity?

2. Until recently, Americans have delegated child rearing to women and breadwinning to men. In what ways can fathers be decisively involved in the rearing of their children?

3. What are some positive behaviors that fathers, and men in general, can model for youth?

4. What constitutes a good male role model?

5. What should parents, teachers, ministers, counselors, and other influential adults be teaching boys so that they will grow up to be responsible men and fathers?

6. What can women do to encourage men to practice responsible behavior toward themselves and their children? How can women discourage irresponsible behavior?

7. What role does the church play in redeeming men? Do you know of effective ministries that empower men to be strong and responsible?

8. Why do so many churches attract more women than men? What changes need to be made to correct this trend? Consider the special needs and tendencies of men as you answer this

question. Think of churches that do a good job of attracting men. What are they doing to attract men?

9. President Clinton has said that welfare reform should include measures to encourage fathers to support their children. The denial of benefits for subsequent children to mothers already on welfare is one way of trying to force fathers to pay. Do you think this is fair? Why or why not?

10. Present a profile of a positive father whom you know. Explain the characteristics that make him a good father.

Good News for Homosexuals

Romans 8:31-39

Introduction

So far we have looked scripturally at different configurations of the family. We have not engaged in an exhaustive look, just a descriptive look. In examining the issues of our families, many of us fail to mention the unmentionable with which so many of us live. Now it is time to mention the unmentionable, to launch out into the deep, and to address the issue head-on: Does the gospel, the Good News of Jesus Christ, have anything to say to persons who are homosexual and to family members of persons who are homosexual? Or does the Word of God limit itself to those persons who are heterosexual?

I have been the ministerial outcast among many of my colleagues for some fifteen years because I refuse to believe that my God loves only some of his world. My Bible does not say, "For God so loved *some* of the world—or *most* of the world—that he gave his only begotten Son that any *heterosexual* who believes in him . . ." My Bible says *all* the world and *whosoever*—not those I like. *Whosoever*—not those who are like me. *Whosoever*. I refuse to limit my God, to lock God into my cultural understandings because culture is fickle. And culture is often wrong. Culture was wrong about slavery. Culture was wrong about women. Culture was wrong about Africans and Indians, and culture was wrong about Christ. I refuse to limit my God, to lock God into little cultural prisons, no matter how comfortable those prisons may feel. I refuse to leave my brain at the door when I come into God's presence to worship or when I read God's Word. And because I refuse, I have been the pariah among many of my clergy colleagues who somehow see me as defective or not quite saved because I won't join them in their homophobic gay bashing and misquoting of Scripture.

I got into a heated argument with a preacher one Sunday morning as I was preparing for worship service. He asked what I was preaching about during Family Month, and I gave him all eight sermon topics in this book. And when he heard the last two topics, "Good News for Homosexuals" at the 8:00 A.M. service and "Good News for Single Folks" at 11 A.M., he said, "I'll be praying for you at eleven, Reverend." I asked, "Why only at eleven?" He said, "You know I have a problem with those homosexuals." And I fired back, "Yeah, I know. I just wonder why you don't have a problem with being married and sleeping with women other than your wife."

I know I'm in a mine field because I know what an emotional subject this is and how unreasonable people become when you start talking about something that makes them uncomfortable. I might as well be at a Ku Klux Klan rally talking about the dignity and worth of African Americans. Klan folk don't want to hear that, just like a lot of us don't want to hear anything positive about any folk who are not like us. I've got deacons so homophobic they virtually say, "Look, Reverend, my mind is made up. Don't confuse me with the facts."

The Question of Biology

One preacher friend and I were sitting in a restaurant looking out onto the ocean—a beautiful place. The waves were playfully splashing upon the rocks. The sun was drawing breathtaking designs on the water. Gulls were lazily gliding back and forth in front of the restaurant, squawking hellos in search of food and tidbits. It was the perfect scene. And there we were into it like two alley cats over the subject of homosexuals. (This use of *homo*, incidentally, does not come from the Latin word for "man," such as *homo sapiens*. It comes from the Greek word for "same," as in *homogenous* and *homogenize*. *Homosexual* is therefore simply an adjective meaning "same sex." I was trying to raise with him the question of biology:

What about people who are born homosexual? What about people whom God made that way from creation? How do we read God's Word in light of that biological consideration? And he was arguing me down. "Ain't no such thing. Ain't nobody born like that. People choose to be like that, or somebody turns them out when they're young. That's why you shouldn't have those folk around young people and children."

We were "getting loud and drawing a crowd" in that restaurant, and there was absolutely no convincing him. It's one thing to not know; but to *not* know and not *know* that you do not know—that's an awful thing. And that's where this preacher was. I got so excited during the argument that I knocked over my iced tea and spilled it all over the folks sitting next to us! And people were staring at us and listening to us. "Wright, you're talking crazy," he said. "People ain't born like that. Period. So let's don't try to talk about what God had in God's mind 'cause God ain't done nothing like that." His voice was louder than mine, so he was drowning me out.

Just then I spotted a psychologist who had walked into the restaurant. I knew that he knew the psychologist and respected him, so I said, "There's Dr. Gooden—somebody with a background in the medical field. Why don't you ask him, since you don't want to hear anything I have to say?" "All right, but you keep quiet. Don't you say a thing. You let me do the talking." I agreed. So he called the psychologist over to our table and said, "Doc? Be quiet, Wright. Doc, is there any medical or scientific proof that says a person can be born homosexual?"

And the restaurant got like that E. F. Hutton commercial when the man says, "E. F. Hutton says . . ." and the entire place falls silent as everyone listens to hear the word from the authority. Doc said, "Not only people, Reverend, but animals can be born with an affinity for the same sex. Of course, Reverend, science has known that for years." My friend looked over at me to see if I was prompting the doctor, and I was staring up at the ceiling. I reminded him: "You told me not to say a word, and I didn't! Now do you believe me?"

Sometimes people can hear things better when the same thing you've been trying to get them to hear comes from some other person who is not as emotionally involved in the conversation as you are. Now that doesn't always work. I know one couple who are on their fourth counselor because the first three did not say what one spouse wanted to hear. One wanted the other told off, and the counselors kept saying, "It isn't all your mate's fault. You have some tree trunks in your eyes that we have to get out before you start trying to extricate that splinter from your mate's eyes." The counselors were dispassionate third parties, not emotionally wound up in the disagreement, but the headstrong mate still didn't want to hear it. Counseling does not always work, but sometimes people can hear things better when the same thing you've been trying to get them to hear comes from some other person who is not as emotionally involved.

When it comes to homosexuality, this question of biology is a stubborn one. John Kinney, dean of the School of Theology at Virginia Union Seminary, and I preached the citywide revival in Pittsburgh for two years in a row. Some preachers there would argue with me every night. John Kinney said, "Jeremiah, you aren't going to convert these brothers. Why don't you just back off?" And I said, "I can't back off because, John, I have sat in my office and had a young woman say to me, 'As you know, I was born a lesbian. (She and I had talked about her sexuality for a number of years.) And, Reverend, the reason I'm in your office today is that I have been gang raped.' A bunch of men picked her up, dragged her into a car at gunpoint, took her over by the interstate, gang raped her for about four hours, and then kicked her out of the car. She made her way to a nearby hospital and called her mama. Her mama came to the hospital. 'All I wanted my mother to do was hug me and tell me it was gonna be all right,' she said, 'but she wouldn't touch me because I'm a lesbian.' So I can't sit in my office and empathize with her and love her as a pastor and then get out here in another city and deny her in front of these brothers."

There is the stubborn question of biology: the selection of sex chromosomes within the fertilized ovum, then the influence upon the embryo and the fetus that goes on within the mother's body. A Johns Hopkins University study says a deficiency or excess of maternal hormones, viral invasion, intrauterine trauma, nutritional deficiency, toxicity, and so forth can influence a person's sexual orientation in the embryonic stage.[1] The hormones that the fetus produces also play a role in the child's sexual development.

These may be influenced very subtly by many seemingly unrelated occurrences. The fetus is not developing in an impersonal environment, in a laboratory somewhere. He or she is living inside a human being who is subject to many internal and external stresses. There is the question of biology.

The Question of Psychology

What happens to the fetus when the mother is chronically angry, chronically depressed, chronically under stress, or chronically overtired? What about the influences of medications, tobacco, alcohol? And lest any mommies start having a guilt trip laid on them because of what may or may not have happened while their homosexual child was in the womb, there is also the matter of psychology.

A very important little volume that every Christian should read is titled *My Son Eric.*[2] This book is written by a Christian woman, Mary Borhek, who has grown by leaps and bounds both in the Word of God and in the field of science. She has come to grips with her son's homosexuality. In one of the best passages in a book chock full of great passages, she writes that she as a Christian has been taught, like most of us have been taught, that homosexuality is an illness, homosexuality should be punished, homosexuality is caused by family configurations, homosexuality results from the way a child responds to his or her particular environment. Homosexuality is a deliberate physical choice, a choice of sin; homosexuality is demon possession; homosexuality is an abomination before the Lord. She thought just like we've been taught, and she tried to figure out what she had done to cause her son to be that way.

I've talked to countless parents wrestling with that same question. What did I do? How did I cause this? Some of them want to leave the church because church people are so ugly and vicious about homosexuals. Now, some of us in the church will tolerate anything heterosexual: adultery, fornication, divorce, promiscuity, prostitution, sadomasochism, rape, incest, child molestation, as long as it's with somebody of the opposite sex. But we get livid and rabid when same-sex issues come up. We will tolerate a man beating his wife or cheating on his wife quicker than we will tolerate two people of the same sex whose commitment to each other means never dishonoring their partner with either violence or infidelity. Church folk are funny that way.

And where church members have been psychologically and morally, as parents of homosexuals, this mother was until she began reading. She tells of having to rethink all of her carefully formed premises and opinions after the shock of learning of her son's homosexuality. And that's what we do. We carry this neat little list of assumptions into every discussion and exploration of a subject that we find distasteful. A friend of hers who was studying child psychology gave her a little book to read. In her chapter, "Man and Woman, Boy and Girl," Mary says that the first page of that book demolished the neat little structure that she had put together in her head. The author said:

> In the theory of psycho-sexual differentiation it is now outmoded to juxtapose nature versus nurture, the genetic versus the environmental, the innate versus the acquired, the biological versus the psychological, or the instinctive versus the learned. The basic proposition should not be of the colonization of genetics and environment, but their interaction. It is not an either-or reality, in other words, but a both-and reality. It is both a question of biology and a question of psychology.[3]

What we are talking about here (and we cannot exhaust such a complex topic in one sermon) is cause. And the Bible is silent on the subject of cause. That's why my preacher friend and I were at such odds in that restaurant—because the Bible does not say anything about people who were made that way from the womb. Why would God create somebody to be doomed to hell before he or she was born? There are no glib answers you can give to such an important set of questions.

When it comes to homosexuality, there is the matter of psychology and of biology, the interaction between *psyche* and *soma*—mind and body. What about the stubborn reality that each person enters into life with a particular set of physical and mental givens that are shaped by the individual circumstances of his or her inheritance? God did that. Or do we stop believing Psalm 100:3 (KJV), "It is he that hath made us, and not we ourselves"?

What about the stubborn given of Christian research—research done by God-loving, Bible-believing, blood-bought, Spirit-taught, tongue-talking, straight-walking followers of Jesus Christ who have demonstrated that a person's entire sexual adjustment in life can be influenced greatly or less greatly by an uncounted multitude of factors beyond anyone's conscious control? How do you square that with those equally stubborn Bible verses about homosexuals that get whipped out on us every time the subject comes up? Let me submit to you three considerations.

We Need to Study Scripture Carefully

First of all, we need to approach our study of the Scriptures concerning homosexuality as prayerfully and as thoroughly as we approach our study of the Scriptures concerning slavery. Racists tried to use, or misuse, certain texts taken out of context to justify holding black folks in chattel slavery. Just as we study those Scriptures carefully and put them up against the whole counsel of God, we need to do the same with the Scriptures on homosexuality. Whether they are in Leviticus, Corinthians, Romans, or Genesis, we need to study the text in *context*, lest we be guilty of the same heresy Jehovah's Witnesses commit when they base their entire argument and understanding on some false pretext.[4]

We need to understand the issues of pederasty and sacred prostitution that were prevalent in biblical days. We need to understand that a lot of what I saw in the Marine Corps also went on in Bible days, when the military victors would turn their vanquished enemies into sexual victims, male and female, as a statement of how little they thought of them. When the Marines hit a village in Vietnam, some would have sex with anybody—man, woman, boy, and girl—to show how little they thought of them. That same behavior is recorded in the Bible, too.

We need to understand the issues at stake in the biblical background before jumping to modern conclusions based on ancient assumptions. We need to walk slowly through the passages that are always trotted out before us to see what it is God is saying.

We Need a Guide

Next, when walking through a mine field, any soldier will tell you that you'd better have a map or a guide. And it is best to have both. There are too many good guides out there for you to try to make it through this mine field alone. Use one of the guides.

Mary Borhek's chapter titled "New Paths through the Desert" is an important guide. She takes you text by text, issue by issue, step by step. Let me just whet your appetite with a paragraph or two from that chapter. She argues that we need to understand that "morality is much more complex and demanding a discipline than mere outward conformity to a list of rules." She says:

> It is possible that the church has come as far as the old path of outward rules will take it in this desert. If so, then new paths must be found. And they will be discovered as we look at what science is demonstrating and bring the deeper meanings of the Bible to bear upon this new knowledge. . . .
>
> This may mean . . . a new searching for the nuggets of gold, the divine truths, those things necessary for salvation that are contained in God's Word. This may seem a risky venture to those who may feel more comfortable with the known boundaries of definite rules. It may even seem to them that we are throwing out the Word of God in favor of the word of science. But it is well to remember that the Church initially rejected Copernicus and Galileo, discovering that the earth revolved around the sun and not vice versa. . . .
>
> They put them out of the church, excommunicated them! God's truth is sometimes so much greater than we want to allow it to be. Who knows? Perhaps God is confronting the church with the present crisis over homosexuality.[5]

And, I would add, the crisis over sexuality in general, because some of us Christians can't deal with *homo*sexuality because we can't deal with *sexuality*, *homo* or *hetero*. Period!

Perhaps God is confronting the church with the present crisis over sexuality. You *do* realize that AIDS is everybody's concern, don't you? Perhaps God is confronting the church not in order to demolish the church but in order to say "grow or die." Our impasse (or our extremity) may be nothing more than God's offering us new and life-giving opportunities to expand and understand these ancient Scriptures. Mary Borhek is a good guide.

Tony Campolo is also a good guide. His book *Twenty Hot Potatoes Christians Are Afraid to Touch* is also a helpful guide.[6] Get a guide, and then use the map to make it through this mine field.

The Question of Theology

Beyond the question of biology, beyond the matter of psychology, is the overriding fact of theology. Behind the text is a theology, and it is this theology that brings good news for homosexuals.

Theology says not to forget love. Read Connie Stark's testimony in the appendix.[7] She said Kenny (her homosexual brother) loved Anita Baker, Luther Vandross—so do y'all, and so do I. But Kenny also loved the Lord. And guess what? The Lord loved Kenny. He gave his Son for Kenny, like he gave his Son for you and me. He gave his life for Kenny, like he gave it for you and me. He shed his blood for Kenny, just like he shed it for you and me. God doesn't get caught up in our hang-ups.

Theology says the same thing to gay folks and lesbian folks that it says to black folks and brown folks. God doesn't make junk. And God doesn't make mistakes. The way God made you is the way God loves you. Theology puts a God perspective on a human situation. Theology reminds us that an adjective is not a noun. I am a black person. *Person* is the noun. *Black* is the adjective. The adjective describes one aspect of my persona. But I have other aspects. I am also old. I am also intelligent. I am also educated. And there is a difference between being educated and being intelligent. I am also a thinking person. I am also an analytical person. I am also a happy person. I am also a hopeful person. I am also an optimistic person and a realistic person. There are many adjectives that describe me. *Greying. Comical. Bad. Fine. Cute. Smooth. Graceful.* Don't limit me to one adjective, because behind the adjective I am still a person. And the same principle applies to homosexual persons. *Homosexual* is the adjective. *Person* is the noun. And as a person I am made in the image of God. Don't try to lock me into one aspect of my persona.

Several years ago Jim Forbes[8] put it this way: "See my mole? Yes, I have a mole. But I'm more than this one mole. Don't make my mole the sum total of my existence." Theology puts a holy perspective on a human situation.

Above the question of biology and beyond the matter of psychology is the overarching issue of theology. And theology has a lot to say about morality and discipleship, ethics and ethical issues, right and wrong. Please remember that everything black ain't beautiful, and everything gay ain't gorgeous. There's a whole lot of ugly in the heterosexual *and* the homosexual worlds. Theology speaks to relationship, commitment, covenant, purity, and holiness. Theology says, "Above all, do not forget God's love." God's love is a lot greater and a lot more inclusive than we want to allow it to be.

Good News for Homosexuals

Let me end up where Tony Campolo started off on his treatment of this subject. Tony tells of a friend of his who was the pastor of a small church located near a funeral home. Whenever somebody died who did not have a church home, the mortician would call this pastor to come do the funeral. One day he asked him to come do the funeral of a gay man who had died of AIDS. So he went. He said there were about twenty men sitting there staring blankly into space. They barely greeted him, and they never changed their expressions. At the cemetery they stood there motionless and silent. After the casket was lowered and the preacher turned to leave, he looked back and they were still just standing there. Saying nothing. Just staring. He walked back and asked if there was anything he could do to help. And one man asked him to read the Twenty-third Psalm. He said, "When I got up this morning to come to this funeral, I was looking forward to somebody reading the Twenty-third Psalm to me. . . . I figured that they always read the Twenty-third Psalm at funerals."

And so he read, *The LORD is my shepherd; I shall not want. . . . Yea, though I walk through the valley of the shadow of death, I will fear no evil: for thou art with me.*

For over an hour they stayed at that graveside as Tony's friend read favorite passages of Scripture to them.[9]

Other passages of Scripture that I have had to use in providing ministry to HIV-infected persons or those who have full-blown AIDS and to persons who were born with same-sex orientation have included words from Psalms that heterosexual Christians may take for granted! Words that have offered hope and comfort for those with whom I have done ministry include the following:

Psalm 27: *The LORD is my light and my salvation; whom shall I fear? The LORD is the strength of my life; of whom shall I be afraid?* When I read that psalm, I think about how one of my lesbian friends claims verse 10 as her verse. She says, *When my father and my mother forsake me, then the LORD will take me up.*

Psalm 34: *I will bless the LORD at all times. His praise shall continually be in my mouth. . . . O magnify the LORD with me, and let us exalt his name together. I sought the LORD, and he heard me, and delivered me from all my fears* (vv. 1,3-4).

Psalm 37: *Fret not thyself because of evildoers, neither be thou envious against the workers of iniquity* (v. 1).

Psalm 46: God *is our refuge and strength, a very present help in trouble. . . . The LORD of hosts is with us; the God of Jacob is our refuge* (vv. 1,7).

Psalm 51: *Have mercy upon me,* O God, *according to thy lovingkindness: according unto the multitude of thy tender mercies blot out my transgressions. Wash me thoroughly from mine iniquity, and cleanse me from my sin. . . . Create in me a clean heart,* O God, *and renew a right spirit within me. Cast me not away from thy presence; and take not thy holy spirit from me* (vv. 1-2,10-11).

Psalm 90: *LORD, thou hast been our dwelling place in all generations* (v. 1).

Psalm 91: *He that dwelleth in the secret place of the most high shall abide under the shadow of the Almighty* (v. 1).[10]

The men in that story and many others like them are hungry for the Word of God. They know they can't get that Word at most churches. Many churches are too busy being culturally holy to be Christlike helpful.

Another passage whose theology we need to hear as we listen to God's good news for homosexuals is Romans 8:35-39. It also is about God's love, which is greater than your love and my love, wider than our love could ever be and deeper than we could ever comprehend. Now picture these men as described in the story, ostracized by the church, put down by the saints, put out by these holier-than-thou church members, and put up with by insensitive family members. See them standing in this isolated cemetery hearing God's Good News: *Who shall separate us from the love of Christ?* Church folk? Saved folk? Narrow-minded folk? Close-minded folk? Homophobes? Whoremongers? *Who shall separate us from the love of Christ? shall tribulation, or distress, or persecution, or famine, or nakedness, or peril, or sword? As it is written, For thy sake we are killed all the day long; we are accounted as sheep for the slaughter. Nay, in all these things we are more than conquerors through him that loved us.* There is the fact of theology behind the text. Theology says something about God's love. *For I am persuaded, that neither death, nor life, nor angels, nor principalities, nor powers, nor things present, nor things to come, nor height, nor depth, nor any other creature, shall be able to separate us from the love of God, which is in Christ Jesus our Lord.* Nothing. Not who I am. Not who you *say* I am. Nothing. Not your opinion of me or my oppression. Nothing. Not holier-than-thou hypocrites. Not saints. Nothing shall separate us from the love of God which is in Christ Jesus our Lord. That's the Good News.

You don't sit high enough to see low enough to dare to presume to judge another one of God's children. That's why Jesus taught that crash course in stone-dropping over in John 8. We all need to examine ourselves and throw ourselves on the mercy of heaven's court and ask God to have mercy. You know, Lord, whether I'm right. You know, Lord, whether I'm wrong. You know, Lord, whether I'm right or wrong.

Devotional

Songs of Praise
Prayer
Scripture: Romans 8:31-39
Song: "Nothing but the Blood of Jesus"

Study Questions

1. What are your views on homosexuality? Are persons born homosexual, do they choose to be homosexual, or are there some in both categories?

2. Do you accept homosexual persons as friends? As acquaintances?

3. Have you ever participated in jokes that ridiculed homosexual persons? Would you define yourself as homophobic (afraid of homosexual persons)?

4. Should the church challenge sexual practices between consenting adult homosexuals? Are these practices any better or worse than illicit sexual practices among consenting heterosexuals, such as fornication and adultery?

5. Are abstinent or celibate homosexual persons all right? In other words, is it all right to be a homosexual as long as one doesn't practice homosexual sex?

Note: Questions 6-9 are designed for personal reflection and are not necessarily intended for group discussion.

6. Are you homosexual? Have you been "in the closet" about your homosexuality? If so, why?

7. Do your family, friends, and other significant others accept your homosexuality? Do you rely on the support of your family and friends to feel good about your homosexuality, or are you able to feel good about yourself regardless of their opinions?

8. As a homosexual, do you think you need to be healed or changed so that you can be heterosexual? Do you think you are normal or abnormal?

9. As a homosexual, how would you like for your church to

respond to you? Do you want your church to perform marriages between homosexuals? Do you want your church to openly ordain homosexual ministers?

10. In your own words, say what the "good news" for homosexuals is. Do the biological and psychological considerations discussed in this sermon help you to see homosexuality differently? Do they matter at all, or does only the theological consideration discussed here truly matter?

Appendix

Connie Starks, a member at Trinity United Church of Christ, shared the following testimony (which has been edited for publication) from her personal diary during one of our Sunday worship services:

Christmas 1990 was a regular, good-old Christmas for my family. New Year's Day we all had dinner together. Dr. King and my stepfather share the same birthday, so we celebrated that, too.

Sometime between King's birthday and January 28, my thirty-two-year-old brother got a cold he couldn't shake. He and his roommate tried everything from aspirin to homemade chicken soup, but Kenny just got worse. He went to the doctor, who said he had strep throat. He went back to the doctor [again when he didn't get better], and the doctor said he had bronchitis. On January 28 my brother was admitted to Rush Presbyterian–St. Luke's Hospital. His roommate told me he had pneumonia in both lungs. I was very upset by this news. I had been concerned about my brother for a while: he had not had a girlfriend since high school, and he had had the same male roommate for about ten years. Now he was very sick. I just felt like crawling in a hole and dying.

On January 29 my mother, Vivian Foster Davis, and I got up, got dressed, and at 11:00 A.M. were at the hospital when visiting hours started. On the way to the hospital, I tried to prepare my mother for whatever I could. We got our visitors' passes and went up to Kenny's room. He was in a beautiful, private room on the eighth floor. He was in good spirits; he was also on 100 percent oxygen. He was scheduled for a test on the fluid in his lungs, so we only spent a few minutes with Ken that day.

But I couldn't hold in my question any longer, so I asked him, "Kenny, do you have AIDS?" He looked over his glasses at me like he did when he was about three years old when I would ask him where his shoes were, and he said, "I don't know, but it's possible." With that, they wheeled him off for his test.

The next day I went to visit Kenny. He really didn't look any better, but he didn't look real sick, either. We laughed and talked—the usual hospital-room conversation. Then Kenny said to me, "We have never talked about my lifestyle. Why?" I said, "I guess because you have always been so private about your life. You always kept your friends and your roommate away from us, the family. So I guess out of respect for you, we have never intruded into that part of your life." He then began to share things with me, things he liked to do, things he *did* do.

Kenny had worked at Rush Presbyterian since he was sixteen years old, and by now he had a hospital family as well. He was the EKG supervisor on the evening shift and a third-year nursing student. He had people visiting him all times of the day and night. Surprisingly, they all knew about his big sister—me—and how I used to keep him in line and get on him about finding his glasses and his shoes in the morning because I had to drop him off at the baby-sitter's on my way to school.

On Thursday, January 31, I talked to Kenny in the morning and told him I would be at the hospital later that evening. He was expecting the results of his test at any time. It was about 2:00 P.M. when the telephone at my beauty salon rang. I answered it, and the voice on the other end said, "The fat lady done sung and she ain't happy." I could hardly make out what he said. It was the kind of voice that Kenny had when he was in trouble or when he would come into my bedroom crying about breaking his glasses again for the tenth time in one year. Anyway, the fat lady singing was something that the two of us shared about bad news and trouble. I told Kenny I would be there as soon as I finished with the client I was working on. I called my cousin, Deborah, who also worked at Presbyterian, and asked her to meet me at Ken's room at three when she got off.

She was there when I got there. A hospital chaplain came in to talk to us about the support group the hospital had for AIDS victims and their families. I think I stayed at the hospital until about nine that night. I was scared to go home and tell my mother that Kenny had AIDS. I told Kenny, "Don't worry. I'll tell mama." I got home, and I told her. And what did she say? "Trust in the LORD with all thine heart; and lean not unto thine own understanding. In all thy ways acknowledge him, and he shall direct thy paths" (Proverbs 3:5-6, KJV).

On February 1, I called Ken bright and early to tell him I would be out later that evening because I had to work. When I got to the hospital, Ken already had company. After I was introduced, we sat around and laughed and talked. I got to see a part of my brother's life I had never known. I heard about the cooking that I had never really sampled. Sometimes he would make some butter cookies and bring them by, but I'm talking about seven-course meals served on china. Vacation trips were another part of his life I had never shared with my brother. Later on that evening, Kenny suffered some kind of anxiety attack, and he was sedated so he could get some much-needed rest.

On Sunday, February 3, I took my mother and stepfather to visit Ken and spent much of that afternoon with him. Ken was still on oxygen. His hospital family stopped by during their lunch breaks and break times. Some of Ken's friends came by, so my mother got to meet them and share in their delightful company.

On Monday, February 4, Ken was scheduled to take another AIDS-related test, but it was canceled because he was too weak. When I visited with him, he seemed somewhat depressed. Mind you, he was a medical professional. He had seen what AIDS could do to an individual. His doctor came by that day. I asked him why

Ken was still on 100 percent oxygen, and he informed me that Ken also had developed emphysema. When they took him off the oxygen, he had had such a hard time breathing that they decided the oxygen was what was best for him.

I visited him every day. My girlfriend, Andrea, went with me for support almost every day. We laughed the whole time we were there with Ken but barely talked to each other on the way home. See, we used to send Ken to the store to get us some salt-and-sour potato chips when Andrea was pregnant with her son, my godchild, who is now twenty-one.

Tuesday, February 12, I returned home after being at the hospital for a good portion of the day. It was about nine when the phone rang. It was one of Ken's friends, Felicia, from work. She was calling to tell me Ken had suffered cardiac arrest. He wanted me to come to the hospital because they were going to have to perform a tracheotomy, which meant that he would be on life support while the doctors performed the surgery.

Deacon Hugh Brandon drove me to the hospital that night. When I got there, Ken had already been sedated and the trach tube had been put in. Ken was going to be moved to intensive care. The staff nurses were just wonderful. Everyone loved Kenny. I think this was the first time I fully realized just how sick Ken was. He had told me that he had never seen anyone come off a respirator alive—but I somehow thought Ken would.

Ken spent the next two weeks in intensive care. He had kidney failure, which caused his body to swell; another kind of pneumonia developed; his lungs collapsed. But this boy never gave up. On several occasions they called me to the hospital, saying this was it. They brought in new medicines from the disease control center in Atlanta, medicines that had not been released—but the doctors have what they call a last attempt at life, and they sent the medicines for that purpose. Ken could no longer talk to us because of the trach tube, so he held conversations with us by writing. He had a list of questions for the doctors when they came in; in fact, he told them about the new medicine at the Atlanta disease control center, and they helicoptered it in.

Friday, February 22, my daughter, then a student at Clark Atlanta University, came home. She had a special relationship with her Uncle Kenny. She used to tease him that she would graduate from college before he did because he was a full-time, all-the-time student. My mother and I picked her up at the airport, and we went right to the hospital. By now Kenny was so sick that we were allowed to visit anytime we wanted. I had spent many hours and days there, and the nurses knew me by name. Kenny's spirits lifted when he saw Dakira.

But we were not the only family members around Kenny's bedside. Ken's room was always filled with family members. Two of my cousins worked at the hospital, and they were always in and out of his room. Doctors and nurses who had worked with Kenny always stopped by to check on him and his condition. Everybody would say something just absolutely wonderful about his character.

Ken had a love for God. He had expressed that in his many visits with Rev. Dawkins when he would stop by to speak with him. He also loved Anita Baker and Luther Vandross—and was probably the only person you'll ever see in intensive care listening to cassettes of their music.

One of the doctors told us that they had done just about all they could for Ken. His heart had suffered a lot of damage, but it was still young, and his brain wouldn't send a message to his heart to stop. By now we knew that the medicine from the disease control center wasn't working. He had been on a morphine drip for five days. The doctors also told us that ordinarily a person has about five hundred T-cells, but at this point Kenny only had two. T-cells are the immune cells, meaning that there was nothing left in his body to fight with.

The doctors began talking about taking him off of the life support. We had a family meeting in one of the hospital rooms. I think seven of us were in that room. Ken had not been conscious in two days. The doctors could do no more for him. We, his family, were suffering because when Ken first found out he had AIDS, he stated emphatically, "I don't want any kind of life support"—and he had been on life support for two weeks. But we weren't God, either, and we couldn't just pull the plug and let our brother, nephew, uncle, and son we all loved go. So the doctors told us that they would unplug a machine that was called a "bird," which made his lungs work. They explained he might die instantly, or it might take a while, but he would be comfortable. So they unplugged the machine—and there was no immediate result. I guess we all sighed with relief.

I must have stayed around the hospital until about ten that night. I think I went home and prayed myself to sleep. I think that's about all I could do at this point. Sometimes they were angry prayers; sometimes they were prayers asking for comfort. I think God was the only One who could understand how hopeless I felt. I called the hospital every night before I went to sleep, and I called about two every morning. Then I called again when the shift would change to see who his morning nurse would be. Nurse Barb informed me that he had made it through the night, but his breathing had become very faint.

My entire family got to the hospital the morning of February 26 and gathered around Ken's bed. Rev. Dawkins was there with us. He and Ken had developed a close, sincere relationship. My aunt left the hospital, saying she wanted to go home. Ken left us shortly after that. It was about noon. I guess we were all pretty much comforted with Ken being at rest.

It was the longest twenty-eight days of my life. We made the necessary arrangements, and Kenny was buried. My family and I were devastated by the effects—how quickly AIDS had destroyed my brother's body and how we had missed parts of his life because we had never acknowledged his lifestyle.

My prayer is that those who have a gay or lesbian or drug abuser in their family might rally to their support and accept their lifestyle before it's too late. My message to you, and the point of sharing this with you, is: Don't waste your time getting hung up on how your loved one got the disease. Concentrate on your loved one. The fact is that the way things stand today, someone you know is going to die from the dreaded disease, as did Kenny, and these may be your last moments together.

Notes

Good News for Married Folks

1. Genesis 35:22; 49:1-4; 1 Chronicles 5:1.

2. Genesis 39:6b.

3. Val Jordan and his wife are leaders of the Married Couples Enrichment Ministry at Trinity United Church of Christ in Chicago, where I serve as pastor. They have been married for forty-seven years and have raised five children and put all of them through college and graduate school.

4. Jeremiah, Sr., and Mary Henderson are my parents.

5. Genesis 41:51.

6. Ephesians 5:21.

7. Dr. Samuel Proctor is pastor emeritus of Abyssinian Baptist Church in Harlem.

8. Genesis 2—3.

9. Genesis 41:52.

10. Asenath, Joseph's wife, was the daughter of Potiphera, the Egyptian priest of On. On (the Greek name is Heliopolis) was the seat of worship of the sun god, Ra, and was one of the most ancient Egyptian cities. See Genesis 41:45.

11. Genesis 41:39-44.

12. The Reverend Walter Scott Thomas is the pastor of New Psalmist Baptist Church in Baltimore and is a popular revivalist.

13. The Hampton Ministers Conference is an eighty-five-year-

old conference held annually at Hampton University in Hampton, Virginia. It is an interdenominational gathering of African American clergy persons, church lay leaders, Christian educators, and musicians who come together to worship, study, and learn. The conference is held each year during the first week of June.

14. Hebrews 11:1 (KJV).

15. Romans 1:17 (KJV). See also Habakkuk 2:4; Galatians 3:11, and Hebrews 10:38.

16. John 11:25 (KJV).

17. Isaiah 11:10; Romans 15:12.

18. John 10:14 (KJV).

19. John 14:6 (KJV).

Good News for Single Folks

1. Terry McMillan, *Waiting to Exhale* (New York: Viking Penguin, 1992).

2. Trinity United Church of Christ in Chicago.

3. 2 Kings 3:11.

4. *The Scarlet Letter*, written by Nathaniel Hawthorne in 1850, was the first American tragic novel. The work tells the story of Hester Prynne, a young married woman in a Puritan New England town, who gives birth to an illegitimate girl while living apart from her husband, Roger Chillingworth. When Chillingworth returns and finds that his wife has been made to wear the letter A in scarlet on her dress as punishment for her illicit affair, he becomes obsessed with finding the identity of her lover. When he finally discovers that his wife's lover was Arthur Dimmesdale, a devout young minister, Chillingworth badgers the already guilt-ridden Dimmesdale, who eventually makes a public confession and dies an untimely death as a broken man. Chillingworth is also destroyed by his own vengefulness, but Prynne emerges relatively unscathed, believing that the adulterous act was consecrated by the deep love that she and Dimmesdale had for one another. She makes plans to leave New England to rear her daughter in Europe.

5. "Softly and Tenderly," Will L. Thompson.

6. This Arabic benediction used by the Islamic religion means "Peace be unto you."

7. "The Fruit of Islam" is the name given to male members of the Nation of Islam and the military training that they undertake.

8. The Qur'an is the Islamic sacred scripture.

9. The Latin expression "quid pro quo" means "something given or received for something."

10. "Lord I'm Coming Home," William J. Kirkpatrick, 1892.

11. This is an old gospel song from the African American church tradition.

Good News for Good Parents

1. "Cousins" is a name given by single mothers to their boyfriends to legitimize the men's constant presence in the family's life. The old slang saying in the African American community "You can't miss what you can't measure" means that you cannot measure whether you have given away love or sexual favors; therefore, you can't physically miss what you can't physically measure.

2. These three couples are members of Trinity Church. Val and Ethel Jordan are an elderly couple who lead the Married Couples Enrichment Ministry. They have been married for forty-seven years and have put all five of their children through college. Mike and Cheryl Brown are a young couple, both of whom grew up in Trinity. They have finished college and graduate school, and, after having lost one child at birth, have had two more and are still faithful church members. Michael and Carol Jacobs are another young couple in their late thirties. They are foster parents and have lovingly cared for their teenage daughter ever since she was born.

3. The BTU (Baptist Training Union) is not held in most Baptist churches anymore, but it was still prevalent through the 1960s and was typically held at church on Sunday evenings. On Sundays, the faithful church member was expected to attend Sunday school in the morning, morning worship church service, any special afternoon services, and BTU in the evening. BTU focused on leadership training and church doctrine.

4. Pierre, Elizabeth, Brenda, Janet, Jeri, Denise, and Leslie are good parents who are members of Trinity Church.

5. Mark 9:38.

6. Luke 9:51-56.

7. Mark 3:17.

8. *Schwartze* is the Yiddish word for "nigger." It is from the German word *schwärze*, which means "black."

9. Dr. Jawanza Kunjufu is a consultant on the education of African American youth and the author of a number of books, including volumes one and two of *Countering the Conspiracy to Destroy Black Boys* (Chicago: African American Images, 1985).

10. The popular forty-five RPMs (revolutions per minute) were small record disks, slightly larger than today's compact disks. They were double-sided, with one song on each side.

11. "Cherry Pie," a hit single during the rock-and-roll era, was sung by a duo named Marvin and Johnny. "Cherry" was a slang term for the female hymen, so "Cherry Pie" was sexually suggestive.

12. Benjamin Carson, M.D., an African American neurosurgeon, successfully performed the first separation of Siamese twins during a twenty-two-hour operation on the Binder Siamese twins in 1987. He was thirty-three years old at the time and director of pediatric neurosurgery at Johns Hopkins Hospital in Baltimore, Maryland. Though he is internationally acclaimed as a great and innovative surgeon, he has endeared himself to many because he is a God-fearing man who is genuinely humble and compassionate. His autobiography is told in *Gifted Hands* by Ben Carson with Cecil Murphey (Grand Rapids: Zondervan Books, 1990).

13. *The Reverend Willie Taplan Barrow* was unique as an ordained woman minister during the civil rights era. She was active with the Southern Christian Leadership Conference and Operation Breadbasket. Presently, she is the national chairperson of the Board of Operation PUSH and an assistant pastor at the Vernon Park Church of God in Chicago.

Mae C. Jemison, M.D., was the first black female astronaut at the National Aeronautics and Space Administration (NASA). In 1992, she boarded the shuttle Endeavor for a one-week mission to study the effects of zero gravity on people and animals.

Arthur Ashe (1943–1993), U.S. tennis player, humanitarian, and social activist, was the first black man to win a Grand Slam event when he captured the men's singles title at the debut of the U.S. Open championship in 1968. He held thirty-three tournament titles during his tennis career. He also championed social causes: the antiapartheid movement in South Africa, refuge for exiled

Haitians, the plight of inner-city children in the United States, and health education related to HIV and AIDS (the disease that claimed his life). Ashe published an autobiography, *Off the Court* (New York: New American Library, 1981), and the three-volume *A Hard Road to Glory: A History of the African-American Athlete* (New York: Warner Books, 1988). Before his death, he organized the Arthur Ashe Foundation for the Defeat of AIDS.

Michael Jordan led the National Basketball Association (NBA) in scoring for seven seasons and helped the 1991-93 Chicago Bulls become the first team to win three consecutive league championships since the 1950s and 1960s when the Boston Celtics won eight in row. He was the first person to be named "Most Valuable Player" of the NBA finals for three consecutive years.

Thurgood Marshall (1908–1993) was the first black Supreme Court justice. He had a major influence in civil rights legislation during this century as lawyer and chief counsel from 1938 to 1961 for the NAACP. His most famous case was the 1954 landmark *Brown v. Board of Education of Topeka*, which declared racial segregation in the public schools unconstitutional.

Langston Hughes (1902–1967) was a journalist and writer whose works included books for children, humor, librettos, lyrics, drama, radio scripts, and poetry. He was among the most beloved of the Harlem Renaissance poets. Some of his better-known poems are "Mother to Son" and "Harlem," the latter from which Lorraine Hansberry derived the title of her play, *A Raisin in the Sun*.

Muhammad Ali was the first and only boxer to win the heavyweight championship three times. He knocked out Sonny Liston in the seventh round on February 25, 1964. He was known for his extraordinary hand-leg coordination, defensive skills, and fast reflexes. The poetic boxer said of himself that "I float like a butterfly and sting like a bee." He proclaimed himself "the greatest." Crowds flocked to see him both for his boxing skills and for his loquacious and colorful style.

Oprah Winfrey is currently the most popular television talk-show host. She owns her own production company, Harpo Productions, and has for the past several years won the Emmy Award for the best television talk show.

Arsenio Hall, a comedian, hosted a popular late-night variety television show.

Ray Charles is credited with helping to develop the soul sound in popular music. He is a pianist, singer, composer, and bandleader. He has been affectionately billed "the Genius." His hit songs include "What'd I Say" (1959), "Georgia on My Mind" (1960), "Hit the Road, Jack" (1961), and "I Can't Stop Loving You" (1962).

Vashti McKenzie is the pastor of Payne African Methodist Episcopal Church in Baltimore, Maryland. She is the first A.M.E. woman pastor in the twentieth century to be assigned to a major urban or metropolitan congregation. Her congregation has a membership of one thousand.

D. Brown Daniels is one of the staff pastors at Trinity Church and runs the Clinical Pastoral Education Program at Evangelical Health Systems/Trinity Hospital in Chicago. She is a role model in the church whom young African Americans can see and "touch" on a daily basis.

Cynthia Hale pastors the Ray of Hope Christian Church (Disciples of Christ) in Decatur, Georgia.

Johnnie Coleman pastors Christ Universal Temple in Chicago, whose membership is over six thousand.

Wynton Marsalis is the leading African American jazz trumpeter in America. He has a degree in classical music and is an expert in music history as well as one of the leading spokespersons in North America on jazz history. He and I collaborated in the writing of *In This House, On This Day*, the highly acclaimed jazz mass.

Kirk Whalum is a contemporary jazz saxophonist who adds a spiritual and Christian dimension to his performances and recordings.

Stevie Wonder is a socially conscious singer and songwriter whose popularity has spanned more than thirty years. He wrote the song that is officially sung during the annual commemoration of the birthday of Dr. Martin Luther King, Jr.

Ozzie Smith is an associate pastor at Trinity Church and a saxophonist who was a musical mentor to Kirk Whalum during Whalum's teen years.

Cheikh Anta Diop is a noted African historian from Senegal. He is the author of *The Origins of African Civilization: Myth or Reality*

(Chicago: Lawrence Hill Books, 1967). In 1966, he was honored at the World Festival of Negro Arts (Dakar) as "the black intellectual who has exercised the most fruitful influence in the twentieth century." Diop's significant contribution has been the combining of African culture and politics in his writings and his emphasis on the great contributions of Egypt to the origins of culture and science. He has insisted that Ancient Egyptian civilization was black.

Zora Neale Hurston (1891–1960), folklorist, novelist, and anthropologist, was one of the first women novelists to write from what today would be considered a feminist or womanist perspective. In her best-known novel, *Their Eyes Were Watching God* (New York: Harper & Row, Publishers, 1937), she depicts the struggle of her protagonist, Janie, whose desire in life is to overcome certain cultural, gender-based restrictions in order to live life in her own way.

Sterling Brown (1901–1991), one of America's leading poets, came to prominence during the great Harlem Renaissance and was known as the "dean of American poets." He is best known for his poem "The Strong Men."

Terry McMillan, contemporary American woman novelist, wrote the best-selling novel *Waiting to Exhale* (New York: Viking Penguin, 1992).

Spike Lee is the contemporary American filmmaker of such films as *School Daze*, *Do the Right Thing*, *Mo' Better Blues*, the epic *Malcolm X*, and *Crooklyn*.

Paula Giddings, journalist, is the author of *When and Where I Enter: The Impact of Black Women on Race and Sex in America* (New York: William Morrow Co., 1984). She says in this book that the assertiveness and organization of black women has furthered the cause of all women as well as all blacks.

Ivan Van Sertima is the author of several works, including *They Came Before Columbus: The African Presence in Ancient America* (New York: Random House, 1976), *the African Presence in Early America* (New Brunswick, N.J.: Transaction Publications, 1987), and *Blacks in Science: Ancient and Modern* (New Brunswick, N.J.: Transaction Publications, 1983).

James H. Cone is the Briggs Distinguished Professor at Union

Theological Seminary in New York and is the author and coauthor of several books that have shaped black theology. He also is author of *Martin and Malcolm and America: A Dream or a Nightmare* (Maryknoll, N.Y.: Orbis Books, 1991).

John Kinney earned his Ph.D. from Columbia University and Union Theological Seminary in New York. He is the Dean of the School of Theology at Virginia Union University.

14. Five Percenters trace their origin to 1934, when Black Muslims first taught that 5 percent of the black population had knowledge of self, 85 percent had no knowledge of themselves, and 10 percent were the preachers who knew that God was the original black man but kept this knowledge to themselves and taught Christianity instead. Today the Five Percent Nation of Islam call themselves gods and earths of the planet Earth. This means that they believe themselves to be original black man and woman with superior genes and brains. Their function is to teach the 85 percent who are not knowledgeable.

15. Meter singing (long meter, short meter, and common meter) is an African form of hymnody that came into existence around the beginning of the nineteenth century.

16. The call-and-response pattern in religious music of African Americans is a retention of African music and can be seen in songs and chants in the Bible. For example, in 1 Samuel 18:7 the lead singer calls out, "Saul has slain his thousands," and the chorus responds, "And David his ten thousands." Many young people are unfamiliar with traditional sacred call-and-response chants, often called "Old One Hundreds." Around 1800, Africans started taking the words of hymns written by persons such as Isaac Watts, Ira Sankey, and Charles Wesley and setting them to African tunes. The leader would "line out" seven or eight syllables, and the congregation would respond by singing those words in a prearranged tune. The tune could be determined by the way in which the "caller" in the call-and-response pattern sang the first few syllables.

17. *Conscious* is a word that is used to explain the awakening of the black revolutionary and consciousness spirits that emerged in America during the Harlem Renaissance period, when the Marcus Garvey and Pan Africanist movements were born.

18. Hebrews 11:1 (KJV).
19. Psalm 27:1 (KJV).
20. Psalm 46:1 (KJV).

Good News for Blended Families

1. Oedipus, the king of Thebes, who killed his father and married his mother, is the main character in Sophocles' Greek tragedy *Oedipus Rex*. Modern psychology's theory of the "Oedipus complex" is based on this play. The theory explains the desire for sexual involvement with a parent of the opposite sex and an accompanying sense of rivalry with the same-sex parent.

2. The infant Jewish boy was to be circumcised on the eighth day following his birth. Mary and Joseph took Jesus to the temple for this ritual circumcision.

3. Luke 2:25-38.

4. The Hampton Ministers Conference is an eighty-five-year-old conference held annually at Hampton University in Hampton, Virginia. It is an interdenominational gathering of African American clergy, church lay leaders, Christian educators, and musicians who come together to worship, study, and learn. The conference is held each year during the first full week in June.

Good News for Bad Kids

1. The term *chronicler* refers to the person who wrote or retold First Samuel.

2. Rev. Barbara J. Allen is the assistant pastor at Trinity Church.

3. William Gray is a former United States congressman (D-Pa.) who now heads the United Negro College Fund.

4. This is an Arabic greeting, used by the Islamic religion, which means "Peace be unto you."

5. Yahweh (YHWH) is the Hebrew word for God. It means "I AM WHO I AM" (Exodus 3:14). A group of black Jews called the Black Hebrew Israelite Nation uses this name for God and the greeting "*Shalom alechem*," which means "Peace be unto you."

6. "Hotep," a general greeting, is adapted from Egyptian religions, such as Amon-Ra (a sect of the worship of Ra, god of the sun and of creation). The greeting is an abbreviation of "*Imhotep*" and/or "*Ptah-hotep*."

7. "*Kemet*" is the ancient Egyptian word for Africa; it means "land of the blacks."

8. Genesis 22:1-14.

9. Genesis 17:15-17; 21:1-2.

10. Genesis 41:39-44.

11. Exodus 14:21-22.

12. Joshua 6:15-21.

13. B. J. Armstrong, Stacey King, Craig Hodges, and Cliff Livingston are members of the Chicago Bulls' "three-peat" championship team because it was predicted that they would win the National Basketball Association championship three times in a row, having previously won it in 1991-92 and 1992-93.

Good News for Good Fathers

1. These episodes from the life of Joseph are recorded in Genesis 37 and 39—45.

2. Psalm 37:23 (KJV).

3. See Genesis 50:20.

4. Romans 8:28 (KJV).

5. Philippians 3:13-14 (KJV).

6. Genesis 37:23-24.

7. Genesis 39:1-18.

8. Genesis 39:20-23.

9. Genesis 40:23.

10. Job 13:15 (KJV).

Good News for Bad Fathers

1. 2 Samuel 13:1-19.

2. 2 Samuel 13:20-29.

3. 2 Samuel 18:15-16.

4. Derrick Bell was a tenured professor of law at the Harvard University Law School. He took a sabbatical leave of absence to protest the law school's discrimination against women in general and minority women in particular. Professor Bell said he would not return to the school unless it demonstrated its changed policy of sexism by hiring at least one black female professor. Harvard refused for over a year, so Dr. Bell no longer teaches there. He is the author of several books, including *And We Are Not Saved* and *Faces at the*

Bottom of the Well (Basic Books, a division of HarperCollins Publishers, Inc.).

5. On April 29, 1992, a jury in Simi Valley, California, acquitted four white Los Angeles Police Department officers on all but one count of beating Rodney King while arresting him for a moving vehicle violation on March 3, 1991. Because the vicious beating of King was videotaped by an amateur photographer and shown worldwide, the acquittal by the jury in Simi Valley's middle-class white community sparked the worst riot in the United States since the Los Angeles Watts riot of 1965. The riot, which took place in South Central Los Angeles, left fifty-three persons dead and twenty-four hundred injured. Property damage was estimated to exceed $1 billion. The U.S. government indicted the officers, charging that they had violated King's civil rights, and a federal court trial was held in April 1993. Two of the four police officers accused of beating King were convicted, and two were acquitted.

6. Psalm 27:1 (KJV).

7. Psalm 27:14 (KJV).

Good News for Homosexuals

1. Mary V. Borhek, *My Son Eric* (Cleveland, Ohio: Pilgrim Press, 1994).

2. Ibid.

3. Ibid., 111.

4. The most effective way to interpret Scripture is first to pray for understanding and then to consider the full context of a passage. "Contextualizing" is done by asking four basic questions: (1) Who is the speaker in the text? (2) Who is the audience (the one[s] to whom the speaker is speaking)? (3) What is the situation? (4) What do other passages of Scripture say about the subject of this text? (Apply questions 1-3 to the other passages as well.)

5. Borhek, 122-125.

6. Tony Campolo, *20 Hot Potatoes Christians Are Afraid to Touch* (Dallas: Word Publishing, 1988). Campolo also deals with the church's approach to the homosexual issue in his newest book, *Can Mainline Denominations Make a Comeback?* (Valley Forge, Pa.: Judson Press, 1995).

7. See the appendix for the full text of this testimony about a

family's interaction with its homosexual brother and son who became ill with AIDS and subsequently died.

8. Dr. James Forbes is pastor of Riverside Church in New York City.

9. Campolo, 107-109.

10. These Scripture quotes are all from the King James Version.